LIVE FOREVER

by

Mylon Le Fevre

With Christi Le Fevre

"O taste and see that the Lord is good!"

Published by Heritage Builders Books
3105 Locan Avenue, Clovis, California 93619
www.heritagebuilders.com

All songs and photographs used by permission. Special thanks to George Conger for the picture with Greg Allman.

DEDICATION

Mylon and Christi would like to dedicate this book to:

All those living in a dark lonely place, who believe their situation is hopeless. To the prisoners who think their lives behind bars are without purpose, a future and a hope. To the soldiers who fight our battle for religious freedom while searching for freedom themselves. To the broken hearted desperate for love and healing. Jesus came to the earth and sacrificed His life to give you a life worth living.

Jesus said in Isaiah 61:1-2,

"The Spirit of the Lord GOD is upon me,
Because the Lord has anointed me
To preach good news to the poor;
He has sent me to heal the brokenhearted,
To proclaim liberty to the captives,
And the opening of the prison to those who are bound;
To proclaim the acceptable year of the Lord."

ACKNOWLEDGMENTS

Thank you, Christi, for loving me and Jesus but not necessarily in that order. Thank you for the years of constant prayer, encouragement and faith in this vision. Especially the years you wrote, rewrote and reworked the book until it revealed the goodness of God. You are the true love of my life.

Thank you, Kenneth and Gloria Copeland, and Pastors George and Terri Pearsons, for accepting Christi and me into your extended family. Thank you for taking us under your wings and teaching us how to live by faith and walk in love.

Thank you, Eileen Richardson, for your editorial assistance and amazing faithfulness to help us do the will of God. What a wonderful gift from heaven our relationship has been all these years. You are our cherished sister and covenant friend.

Thank you, Gina Lynnes. We honor the anointing on your life and ministry which made the book so much better!

Thank you, Alvin Lee, for being a real friend, a good dreamer and a great guitarist. Thank you for giving me a safe haven at your home in England. Without your friendship and generosity, I'm not sure I would have lived through that dark season of my life.

SPECIAL THANKS TO MY BOARD OF DIRECTORS AND
THE EXECUTIVE PRODUCERS OF THIS BOOK:

Your godly wisdom and abundant generosity is helping to further the Kingdom of God in the earth. Thank you for believing in us and loving us!

Steve and Patricia Floyd	Peter and Summer Furler
Brig and Lita Hart	Charlie and Debbie Kalb
Meurice and Peggy Le Fevre	Eileen Richardson
Bob and Linda Robinson	Corbin and Holly Roush
Frank and Cindy Soucinek	Dr. Stan and Kim Yeatts

ENDORSEMENTS

Every young person and every parent in America needs to read LIVE FOREVER, the life story of Mylon LeFevre. I've known Mylon and Christi for many years. I know firsthand that he tells it straight. He lives it straight, and his new book is a must-read story of the changing power of the Love, the Word and the precious Blood of Jesus. Thanks Mylon!

JESUS IS LORD!
Kenneth Copeland

Mylon's new book is one of the best testimony books I've ever seen — and it's definitely the most professionally produced. But what's most important is the window presented within its pages through which you can observe a life so vividly transformed by Jesus Christ. As I read this book, I kept thinking, What a glorious example of the 'old man' versus the 'new man.' This volume with its marvelous photography tells the story of a life that has been radically changed. And just as Mylon's life was changed, your life can be changed too. Read this book and see what God can do if you'll give Him a chance!

Rick Renner
Senior Pastor, Moscow Good News Church

One of my favorite old songs is, "Noah Found Grace in the Eyes of the Lord." I knew Mylon when he was a kid. I knew his family. I stayed in contact with him when he was in the wilderness and then watched him grow as a new creation in Christ. It's a joy to see how the Lord is using Mylon and Christi in their ministry now. His new book, LIVE FOREVER brings back a lot of memories and reminds me that he has indeed "found grace in the eyes of the Lord."

Bill Gaither
Recording Artist, Producer and Songwriter

ENDORSEMENTS

It's an honor as well as a privilege to recommend Mylon Le Fevre's new book to you. This is a must-read for anyone who wants to see how the Lord can transform a life. Mylon's straight-up honesty is so much like the Apostle Paul. The story of his life is a compelling one that he tells in such a way that gives hope for anyone who will call on Jesus. This is a powerful read that will impact and touch men and women inside prison—whether that prison is a physical one or not.

Mike Barber
President and Founder, Pro-Claim/Mike Barber Ministries

Mylon's journey is captivating. I could not put this book down! I traveled with him from his Christian childhood to his descent into darkness—and finally, to his personal encounter with Jesus. As his pastor, his story deeply touched my heart and will surely touch yours. He is living proof that God's love can resurrect even the most desperate life.

Pastor George Pearsons
Eagle Mountain International Church, Fort Worth, Texas

I became friends with Mylon back in the '70s when we were both trying to survive the hazards of the music industry! Mylon's story is the real deal! From early gospel roots to the King of Rock & Roll, and finally to the King of kings! LIVE FOREVER is an amazing true story of redemption and a must-read for anyone who has lost their way in life's journey!

Caleb Quaye
Original Guitarist for Elton John

ENDORSEMENTS

I have known Mylon Le Fevre for over 30 years, as both his entertainment lawyer and as his friend. I have seen his maturity as a human being, and observed his pursuit of his faith as it changed his life. I believe LIVE FOREVER is a true expression of his life and that others will learn from his experiences. The book is a good read; it is heartwarming, it is human, and it makes one think about what is truly important in one's life.

Joel A. Katz
Greenberg Traurig

I have always sensed the presence of the Divine in my friend, Mylon. He had all the ingredients to be one of the elite rock stars but his calling was always from far beyond the stars.

Allen Toussaint
Rock & Roll Hall of Fame Artist, Songwriter and Producer

ABOUT THE AUTHOR

Grammy and Dove Award-winning musician, Mylon Le Fevre is widely recognized by music historians as one of the most influential forerunners to the Contemporary Christian Music genre. He was born into the legendary gospel-singing family, The Le Fevres. When Mylon was 17 years old, his first song, "Without Him," was recorded by Elvis Presley. Over the next year, 126 artists recorded Mylon's songs. At 19 years old he made his first album and has sold millions since then. His highly acclaimed 1969 album, *"We Believe"* on Cotillion Records, was the first ever to be released by a Christian rock band on a major secular label.

In 2004, Mylon was awarded an Honorary Doctorate from Life Christian University. In 2005, he was inducted into the Gospel Music Association Hall of Fame and in 2007; he was inducted into the Georgia Music Hall of Fame. Today he is a nationally known speaker and teacher of the Word of God. He and his wife, Christi, travel together internationally, ministering in churches, revivals, rallies and crusades. They make their home in Fort Worth, Texas.

FOREWORD

This book is the true story of a simple uneducated kid from Georgia whose dreams all came true. From his lonely, angry childhood, he wrote and sang music as a way to express his deepest feelings. While in the Army, at age 17, Elvis Presley recorded one of his songs which opened doors around the world to castles, stadiums, arenas, movies, TV, etc. From then on his life was a whirlwind-ride of a rock and roll fantasy that he couldn't make up if he tried.

This is Mylon's story, in its entirety, for the first time in print, with over 100 photos, and lyrics to 15 of his most popular songs. From playing stadiums, coliseums and getting high with some of the biggest rock stars in the world, to being strung out on heroin and cocaine, he was trapped in a seemingly hopeless pit of depression and loneliness. It's all here, the good, the bad and the ugly. Mylon finally found what he was looking for, but it wasn't in drugs, money or fame... he found God. Not religion, but rather a loving Heavenly Father who forgave him and filled him with purpose and hope.

TABLE OF CONTENTS

CHAPTER ONE

BRIGHT STARS IN A DARK SKY

HE IS STRONG

What am I gonna do
Too much is going on
Somebody help me please
Can't make it on my own
Voices from my childhood call
My Momma sang a song
Jesus is calling ya'll
Son when you're weak, He is strong

Excerpted lyrics by Mylon Le Fevre
Angel Band Music/Dayspring Music
Used by permission

One of my very first memories on planet earth is looking out the back window of my daddy's 1947 Cadillac. *How could the sky be so dark and the stars be so bright at the same time?* I used to wonder. It was just a kid's question. Nothing deep. I had no idea it captured the story of my future. As a little boy, rocking along every night on those endless, lonely, two-lane roads, watching the white lines disappear under the red glow of taillights, I never dreamed I was headed toward a darkness that would almost destroy me...and a light so bright it would one day save my life.

I didn't think about those things back then. I just took the days as they came. Growing up "on the road," I figured everybody's parents were musicians; that it was normal to eat at a truck stop every night after the gig, then travel to the next town to sing again. Touring with my family from concert to concert, and church to church—from Memphis to Charlotte, Atlanta to Dallas, Tampa to Louisville—I spent most of my childhood crisscrossing the Bible belt of the Old South. I don't suppose there is a little country town with a high school gym or singing hall where my family didn't sing about Jesus.

While other kids' parents bought station wagons, mine bought an old Greyhound bus, took out the seats and replaced them with La-Z-Boy recliners that doubled as beds. Man, I thought that was cool—especially considering our family's rustic roots. In the 1920s, The Le Fevre Trio had traveled by horse and buggy. My father, Urias, my Uncle Alphus, and my Aunt Maude landed their first big break after bouncing 60 miles down a dusty dirt road to sing on the famous Grand Ole Opry radio show. When they finished singing, the show's sponsor, Purina Chow, paid them two live chickens and a 50-pound sack of Purina Chow!

From then on, by bus or by buggy, it seemed the Le Fevres were always going someplace to sing. That's actually how my parents met. My father saw my mother, Eva Mae, for the first time when he went with his Bible school quartet to the North Chattanooga Church of God, in Tennessee. My grandfather, the Rev. H.L. Whittington, was the pastor. Momma, a musical prodigy at 8 years old, had started playing the pump organ at the church when she was so small she needed help to reach the foot pump. She was self-taught on the piano. Daddy decided at this very first meeting, he had met his future wife. He told his brother, Alf, he would marry her as soon as she came of age. Dad stayed true to his word and in 1934 Mom and Dad were married. While they attended Lee Bible College, Mom took Aunt Maude's place in The Le Fevre Trio and sang about heaven until she moved there 75 years later.

In their first years of marriage and music, my parents' future looked as bright as the stars. Daddy saw my mother's exceptional gift for playing piano, singing, and especially for speaking, so he appointed her MC of the group which, at the time, was unheard of for a woman. Dad kept playing and singing and became the group manager. In 1940, they gained some notoriety playing on WGST, a local radio show in Atlanta sponsored by the NuGrape soft drink company.

Then the shadow of World War II fell over the nation and everything changed.

My mother, already busy raising three children, became pregnant yet again with me. Then my father was shipped off to duty in the U.S. Navy. While my dad served our country on a ship somewhere near the Philippines, my mother delivered me at the U.S. Naval Base Hospital on Oct. 6, 1944, in Gulfport, Mississippi. At 26 years old, she managed to raise four small children on her own until Daddy finally came home from the war when I was 2 years old.

At Right: The Le Fevre Trio

The LeFevre Trio
and
Rev. H. L. Whittington

ON THE ROAD AGAIN

With the nation at peace and our family back together again, The Le Fevre Trio expanded. The children—Pierce, Meurice, Andrea, and eventually me—joined in and the group became simply The Le Fevres. Daddy insisted on it. He made all his kids sing, whether they were talented or not. I don't think he believed God would give him a child who couldn't sing. The first time I sang publicly at 5 years old, I was so little I had to stand on the piano bench to reach the microphone!

Even with some of us singing on tiptoe, The Le Fevres' music found an audience. In the 1950s, we began appearing on local TV. Videotape hadn't yet been invented so we broadcast every show live. After performing the show in Atlanta, our family traveled each week to do shows in Augusta, Macon, Columbus, and Savannah, Georgia. Friday and Saturday nights we sang concerts; then we started the whole process over again on Sunday.

When video was introduced, we began taping the broadcasts at Ted Turner's very first TV station in Atlanta. From there, copies of the tapes went out to 126 cities, one at a time, to make our show the first syndicated Christian TV show in the world! Courtesy of Martha White Flour Company, it also became the first Christian show to have national sponsorship. Eventually, the show grew to include three other gospel groups and became The Gospel Singing Caravan with my mom as the MC.

HEALING, HOLINESS, AND HYPOCRISY

The Le Fevres, launched into the spotlight through television, soon became famous in Southern Gospel music. With my mom well on her way to becoming the queen of the genre, our family performed in some of the largest auditoriums and arenas in the country.

We also sang for some of the biggest revival crusades and TV evangelists of the 1950s. During those years of the great healing revival, I watched with utter amazement as God worked mighty miracles through such men as Oral Roberts, A.A. Allen, Rex Humbard, and Jack Coe. Afterward, laughing and playing backstage with their children, I never suspected I'd someday need such a miracle myself.

My family not only sang for truly great ministers of God but also for some ministers who weren't really serving Him with their whole hearts. So I saw a lot of holy stuff and a lot of hypocrisy. I didn't intellectually understand the difference. But, as most children do, I sensed in my spirit that one was right and the other wrong. And like the world war that had once darkened my parents' life, the wrong I saw cast a shadow over mine.

A battle began inside me. Shaken by the good and bad I'd seen existing side-by-side in God's people, I started to question the possibility of ever really walking close to Him.

How can the sky be so dark and the stars so bright at the same time? It started out a kid's question but as the years passed it became a major spiritual dilemma. Although I would struggle with it for decades, when I finally found the answer, it would keep me singing for the rest of my life.

CHAPTER TWO

MUSICAL DREAMS

GOSPEL SHIP

I have good news to bring
And that is why I sing
All of my joy with you I'd like to share
And when my ship comes in
I'm gonna leave this world of sin
I'm going sailing through the air

I'm gonna take a trip
In that good ole gospel ship
And I am going far beyond the sky
And I'm gonna shout and sing
Until all the heavens ring
When I am bidding this ole world goodbye

Good Bye Ya'll
Now don't you want to go with me

Mylon Le Fevre
Angel Band Music/Dayspring Music
Used by permission

God's goodness doesn't always show up in a blaze of glory. Instead, it sneaks up on you. It wraps itself in the ordinary and turns you toward your destiny when you're not looking. At least, that's how it happened to me.

Long before I heard the fanfare of fame, or jammed in castles with millionaire musicians, God's grace set my course on my Aunt Maude's farm. Every Thanksgiving all the Le Fevres gathered there for our family reunion. The farm was heaven on earth for me when I was a kid. It was a beautiful homestead about five miles down a dirt road in the rolling hills outside of McMinnville, Tennessee. My Uncle Othel, and his brother, Homer Parsley, (No city slicker names for us; my family was definitely from the country!) inherited it from their father who divided it between them.

I'll be forever grateful for that farm. For me, playing hide and seek in the hay barn, shooting my BB gun at everything in sight, swimming in the creek, and catching crawdaddies with my cousins, was the best kind of fun. And it got even better when my Uncle George would show up with a box full of firecrackers. Cheap as dirt back then, firecrackers were illegal in Georgia but not in Tennessee. So when Uncle George brought Cherry Bombs, M-80s, TNTs, sparklers, and Roman Candles to Aunt Maude's, we freaked out. We blew up stuff for days and lit up the Southern sky at night.

When the fireworks were over and the grownups were finished playing rook, I'd head for Aunt Maude's attic. That's where I always slept, with three or four of my ornery cousins, under piles of homemade quilts in a big old feather bed. It was the best place on the planet to sleep—with occasional exceptions, of course. Like the time I woke up in the middle of the night and realized nature was calling. Tossing and turning as the rain danced on the tin roof overhead, I debated the risk. It was so cold in that unheated attic and so cozy under all those quilts! When I couldn't stand the discomfort any longer, I finally decided to brave the dark and run as fast as I could in my long johns and boots to the outhouse. It seemed to me, a city boy, to be at least a mile away, but I made it.

Then I had to face the return trip.

That was the scariest part. Terrorized by the thought of unseen spiders, snakes, and other critters crawling around in the pitch dark outhouse and tormented by the sounds of the night creatures outside, I tore back to the house in such a panic that I trampled down the perfect rows of my Aunt Maude's prized tomato patch.

I didn't mean to do it. But every monster that ever chased a 6-year-old in the dark was after me that night! My only goal was to make it to the light on Aunt Maude's back porch alive.

The next day my blunder became blatantly obvious. It looked like a tornado had beelined from the outhouse to the back door. I'd torn up Aunt Maude's precious tomato plants and she threatened to tear up my behind if I ever did it again!

BREAKFASTS, BUCKSHOT, AND BANANA PUDDING

But not even booger bears or Aunt Maude's wrath could dampen the excitement of days on the farm. As I awakened in the mornings, the first breath of that brisk air would jerk me into consciousness just in time to see the sunrise. The only heat in the house radiated from the fireplaces in the downstairs living room and dining room, or from the kitchen where Aunt Maude was cooking on her old, wood-burning stove. Since I was the smallest, survival for me meant getting warm first before my bigger cousins, brothers, and uncles got there and pushed me out of the way. So, as soon as I opened my eyes, the race was on.

Making my way to the kitchen fire, I was greeted by the delicious aroma of sizzling country ham and eggs, and giant biscuits rising in the oven. My momma, grandmother, and aunts had already been awake for hours cooking up a big spread for breakfast. Everything in the meal came straight from Aunt Maude's farm. We devoured fresh eggs from their chickens, country ham from their hogs, and butter they had churned the night before. With ice cold milk from their cows, we washed down homemade biscuits topped with red-eye gravy or sorghum syrup made from their sugar-cane crop.

Then all the men went hunting for the day. I carried my BB gun until I was 12. After that I went to work mowing lawns at 25 cents apiece. That doesn't sound like much now but in 1957 it was enough to help me earn the $16 I needed to buy a 20-gauge shotgun. I never really shot any game but I did enjoy the special camaraderie and bonding time with my dad, brothers, uncles, and cousins. As I grew older, my family endlessly teased me because I never fired my shotgun. I put up with it for years. Then, one unforgettable day when I was about 20, I put a stop to it. I decided while under the influence of some serious "herbs" that I'd had enough of their making fun of me.

Determined to shoot something, I took aim at the next rabbit the dogs jumped. But my buckshot didn't hit the rabbit. It hit one of my family's prized hunting dogs in the behind.

After about three flips, that poor dog never was the same again! Needless to say, my family stayed off my back about shooting animals from then on. I still went hunting with them every Thanksgiving, though. I even bought all the camouflage clothes, gear and boots. But I only fired my shotgun one time in about 20 years.

After those famous hunting trips, famished from tramping up and down the Tennessee hills all day, we returned to another homemade feast, fresh from the farm. We'd gorge again until we were all in pain and Aunt Maude brought out her famous banana pudding. When we were too stuffed to swallow another bite, we'd meander out to the front porch just to breathe and rest while the women cleaned up the kitchen.

PICKIN' ON THE PORCH

That's when the time tested routine, the ordinary moments that would have such an extraordinary effect on the rest of my life, would begin. Somebody would pull out a harmonica, a banjo, or a mandolin, and the magic would start. Because music was at the core of our family, almost every member played some instrument. One distant cousin brought his big bull bass all the way from California, strapped to the top of his old woody station wagon. As everybody began tapping their feet to the hillbilly rhythms on that hollow wooden porch, it sounded like the best drummer in Dixie to me.

The less experienced musicians would start these "picking and grinning" sessions. Once they played for a while, my father, his brother, and the other really gifted players would pull out their axes: fiddles, guitars, twelve strings, mandolins, and an accordion. The result was some of the best Gospel bluegrass music you ever heard.

Good doesn't even begin to describe it. Or then again, maybe it does. There, on Aunt Maude's porch, without any blaze of glory, I heard sounds so good they captured my heart. And in the Tennessee twilight as the stars began to shine, I made a decision that would end up taking me places beyond my wildest dreams: *I'd spend the rest of my life making music.*

CHAPTER THREE

CHURCH BOY

THE POWER

Everybody's running
Where do we think we're going
And what is everybody thinking of
Is that the wind we're chasing
Our memories erasing
Have we denied the power of Love

Don't deny the power
This is the final hour
So don't deny the power of Love

Life is so demanding
And what is understanding?
And can you really, really trust your mind
That's why I'm shouting out the warning
He could be coming in the morning
Are you afraid of what He's gonna find
Please don't deny the power of Love

Lyrics by Mylon Le Fevre
Angel Band Music/Dayspring Music
Used by permission

Most kids don't commit the unpardonable sin in church before they're 10 years old. But I did. Or so I thought. The best I remember, it was a sweltering day in August during a typical Sunday morning service. With no air conditioning to cool things off, funeral-home fans were waving frantically throughout the church. My granddaddy's voice, rising in its familiar, song-like rhythm, had inspired the congregation, and the weekly jumping and hollering had commenced.

The scene was familiar to me. I saw it all the time. But I was caught off guard when one elderly gentleman who usually slept in church woke up. Realizing he hadn't hollered yet, he screamed so loud it scared me right out of my seat. When "hollering-man" screamed, then "running-man" took off around the pews. That was "chicken-woman's" cue to do her thing and all I can tell you is, it was on!

I don't know what her real name was but all of us kids called her "chicken-woman" because when Granddaddy got wound up, she would jump to her feet, whooping with her elbows out like wings, and bob her head back and forth just like a chicken! When I inquired as a child why people did stuff like that in church, the Holy Ghost always got the blame. So the Sunday Momma heard me say "Look out, here comes chicken-woman!" I found myself in major trouble.

Momma told me not to make fun of the Holy Ghost because it was blasphemy. I asked what blasphemy was and she said it was the unforgivable sin. That freaked me out. I thought, *Oh Lord, it's too late, I've already done it!*

I wish I'd known then what I know now: that God is so good, He's already granted forgiveness to anybody who will receive it (including little boys baffled by what they see in church); that the Holy Spirit is wonderful not weird. I guess my parents didn't know how to explain those things to me. Or maybe they thought I was too young to understand. Either way, I left church that day more confused than ever. I knew I needed God's help and desperately wanted to go to heaven instead of hell. But, terrified by the thought of doing "the chicken" in front of my friends, I told the Lord if it was all right with Him I'd just take a pass on that Holy Ghost deal.

ELBOWS AND THE ENFORCER

Truth be told, I would have preferred to skip church altogether in those days. But I didn't have a choice. Since my granddaddy was the preacher, our family had good seats down front in every service—and we were always in them. As the smallest, I sat right next to my mom in case she needed to elbow me to keep me quiet. I knew the routine well: If you got three elbows, then you got "the look" which meant she was going to tell Daddy. If Daddy found out you were acting up in church, you'd better pray fast because you were quickly approaching the valley of the shadow of death. The only scripture I ever remember Daddy quoting was, "If you spare the rod, you spoil the child."

Whether I liked it or not, in my family, going to church was like breathing: Life depended on it.

My grandfather built 39 churches for the Church of God denomination before he finally moved to heaven at 103 years old. My mother, having grown up in the church, determined early on that all of her children would do the same. Even after traveling all week and sometimes all night, she always got home in time to take her children to the house of God. As far back as I can remember our family was there every time the doors opened.

Once Momma made the decision that we were going to church, my daddy enforced it without negotiation. There was no such thing as child abuse in the 1950s and children definitely didn't sue their parents. If a judge had told my dad he couldn't whip his kids, my dad would have whipped the judge!

For years, I went to church not because I loved God, but because my dad was bigger than me. As an angry adolescent, I vowed that when I got as big as my daddy, I wasn't ever going to church again, and nobody was ever going to tell me what to do. I adopted a rebellious attitude that put me on a destructive path and almost cost me my life.

Today, by the mercy of God, I see things differently. I'm very thankful for my parents' commitment to my Christian upbringing. I understand that Mom, the one who first told me about Jesus and taught me to sing for Him, gave me a priceless gift. Her dedication to her children hearing God's Word has produced a tremendous harvest in my life.

SUNDAY SCHOOL BLUES

I don't want to tell you how to live
I don't want to tell you what to give
I don't want to tell you what to do
I got to be me; you got to be you

I'm not trying to tell you I'm right
I'm not trying to tell you you're wrong
I'm not trying to tell anything
I'm just trying to sing my song

I don't want you to accuse
No and I don't want you to refuse
Just want you to love not hate
To try to understand and appreciate

What He's done for me and you
So please don't give me those
Sunday School Blues

Lyrics by Mylon Le Fevre
Angel Band Music
Used by permission

Church Boy

24

Even though I never read the *King James Version* of the Bible, I still quote scriptures from memory in *King James* because of all those years of sitting in church. The Word of God was planted in my heart at a young age and, just as Isaiah 55:11 says, it did not return void.

THE GOSPEL ISN'T BAD NEWS

As grateful as I am for the truth I was taught in church, not everything I learned was right. The "hell, fire, and brimstone" style of preaching I heard there implied that every time you made a mistake, God was going to get you. I guess the purpose was to either scare you out of hell or the hell out of you, whichever came first. It's no wonder I often left church feeling discouraged! It seemed like all I ever heard there was bad news!

As I eventually discovered, the true gospel is just the opposite. Gospel means *Good News* or *glad tidings*. It's the message that **God is a good God! He's not mad at anybody. He is not out to get us, He is out to bless us!**

Because I didn't understand how much God loved me, as a teenager I fell into severe depression. I gave Jesus my sins every Sunday but I never gave Him my life. I asked Him to help me with my problems but I never changed the bad choices I was making every day. I got stuck in a cycle of failure and frustration.

One time when I was about 13 years old, I realized how pointless it all seemed. A youth evangelist preached at our church and, feeling conviction for the sin in my life, I went down front (for about the hundredth time) to "get saved." After I prayed at the altar with the other sinners, asking God to forgive me, the evangelist told us to turn around and face the congregation and the front doors of the church. Then he said, "Now I want you to go to school tomorrow and invite all your friends to church because they really need what we've got."

I remember so clearly looking out at our predominantly poor, oppressed, unhappy congregation and family thinking, *Why in the world would anybody want what we've got?! We're some of the most miserable suckers on the planet! I don't even want what we've got.*

My precious family served God with all the revelation they had. But in my childhood, I rarely saw the joy of the Lord on their countenance or the peace of God that passes understanding ruling their hearts and minds. Instead of really enjoying the abundant life in Christ that He provides, we seemed to just survive day to day.

Yes, our church members got excited on Sunday, but I knew what life was really like for screaming-guy, running-man, and chicken-woman. I could see that all their screaming, running, and even doing the "funky chicken" hadn't set them free or gotten the devil off their backs. Surrounded by sweet, good Christian people, I watched them run to church every time the doors opened to get some relief from the stress and pressure of their lives. Then I watched them return home discouraged, to face reality with very little hope and even less faith.

They were definitely on their way to heaven but they were not enjoying the trip!

In the years since, I've found out why. I've learned that there is nothing wrong with getting excited or having a good time in church. And being filled with and led by the Holy Spirit has raised the quality of my life exponentially. But now I know, God's best comes from simply trusting and obeying Him. As John 8:31-32 says, it's knowing and living the truth of God's Word that will make us free.

Today, as a teacher of the Good News, I understand that God's will for me and my family was and is perfect peace and supernatural, overflowing joy. Jesus came to this earth and gave His life so that my family and yours might "have and enjoy life and have it in abundance (to the full, until it overflows!)" (John 10:10, AMP). **As believers, we should be the most loving, kind, peaceful, patient, joy-filled people on the planet. In fact, I found out: If we're not enjoying being Christians, we simply aren't doing it right!**

CHAPTER FOUR

SCHOOL OF HARD KNOCKS

When my parents dropped me off at Tallulah Falls, I was only 12 years old. A state run boarding school in the north Georgia mountains, it was the hardest, coldest, darkest place I'd ever been.

Unlike the other kids at Tallulah Falls, I didn't end up there because a juvenile court sent me. I didn't go because I was too young (or not considered dangerous enough) for prison. I wasn't an orphan or a runaway fleeing a foster home or a horrible, abusive situation. The only kid at the school whose parents were still alive and married to each other, I was there because my mom and dad couldn't take care of me anymore. They had to send me somewhere and Tallulah Falls was the most affordable place they could find.

For two years, my parents had been under tremendous stress trying to care for my little sister, Monteia. She'd suffered from epileptic seizures ever since she was born. At the time, there was no treatment for her condition. The doctors didn't even understand the problem. All they could do was experiment with possible solutions. My parents ultimately sold everything they owned to ensure Monteia received the best medical care available, but she only grew worse. Ultimately, she was placed in a private home where she could be lovingly cared for 24 hours a day.

As my parents frantically prayed for a miracle and struggled to improve my sister's life, mine fell into chaos and confusion. I needed help but Mom and Dad didn't have time for me. They were consumed with helping Monteia and keeping up their intense traveling and TV schedule. My older brothers and sister couldn't look after me because they were already grown and in college. So boarding school had seemed like the only option.

Because money was so tight, a friend had suggested Tallulah Falls.

I enrolled as the youngest and smallest of about a hundred angry, hurt, and scared young men, ages 12 to 18 years old. From day one, my whole world changed. I started going to bed hungry at night because the bigger guys bullied the smaller kids and took our food. I shivered in the winter because they also stole our warm clothes and blankets. There was nothing I could do about it, either. Appealing to the staff (who couldn't care less) just got you branded a rat. Years of dealing with troubled youngsters had left most of them calloused and uncaring, and even physically, verbally, and mentally abusive.

As a sheltered kid from a Christian family, the harshness of the atmosphere jarred me to the core. I was cursed at daily by the other kids. I lived in constant fear because I had to fight almost every day. I didn't know how to throw a punch but it didn't take me long to figure out what survival required. Realizing I wasn't big or strong enough to win a fair fight, I earned the reputation of being a small kid that you could push around—but it would cost you later...maybe in the dark.

Everything about my first year at boarding school hurt. But what wounded me most was that my parents were only able to visit me once. Traumatized by this perceived rejection, I could hardly believe they would let total strangers control my life. How could they leave me in this place to be slapped again and again by uncaring teachers? Why would they allow me to be bruised and beaten by a sadistic coach with a paddle-shaped weapon he referred to as "the board of education"?

I thought my parents were supposed to care for me, protect me, and help shape my identity. I was too young to understand they were doing the best they could in the toughest situation they'd ever faced. So, feeling utterly abandoned, I came to the painful conclusion there was no one I could count on when the chips were down.

Not even the people I loved the most.

PUTTING A GUN TO MY HEAD

After Tallulah Falls, my parents sent me to the Academy at Bob Jones University in Greenville, South Carolina. A Christian school, it promised a safer, more peaceful environment. I arrived thinking my fighting days were over. But as it turned out, I just exchanged one fight for another. Instead of trying to steal my meals and clothes, at Bob Jones they tried to steal my music.

They referred to the Southern Gospel sounds of my childhood as "Jesus Jazz" because of its syncopated sound and black influence. And, as a segregated school with no black students or staff, they rejected it completely. The day a teacher heard me playing one of my mother's songs in my dorm room, all my parents' gospel albums were confiscated. I was treated as if I had been caught with drugs. Since I rarely got to see my family, listening to their music was the one thing that made me feel close to them. But at Bob Jones University, that didn't matter to anybody but me.

I didn't give up hope, though. I went to my first day of voice class with great anticipation because our teacher had asked every student to audition in front of the class. Others may have been nervous, but I had been singing in front of crowds since I was 5. I believed this one class would be the bright spot in an otherwise depressing place because music was my destiny.

Full of excitement about the future, I sat down at the piano and started to sing one of my favorite Southern Gospel songs. The teacher stopped me before I finished the first verse. After informing me that my style of music was unacceptable, she dismissed me from voice class. (I figured out later that the only style of music deemed acceptable was operatic interpretations of songs from the Broadman Hymnal.)

I left the class in total humiliation, vowing before God that no one would ever stop me from singing my songs again.

The following year I had the chance to keep that vow when my parents came to Greenville to do a concert. They lived only a short distance away in Atlanta in those days, but I hadn't seen them since summer vacation because of their endless travel schedule. Needless to say, I'd missed them and wanted to spend time with them. Because the school opposed their music, I was allowed to attend the concert but forbidden to sing. When I told my dad, he decided that should be his decision and not the school's. So, of course, I sang.

The next day, the Dean called me to his office and kicked me out of school. I was completely devastated. I'd worked so hard to make good grades and please my parents and teachers. Most importantly, I was giving my all to develop my relationship with God. I wasn't trying to make trouble. I was just seeking what every 14-year-old kid on earth needs: love, encouragement, patience, and understanding. If I'd been expelled for lying, stealing, drinking or getting stoned, I would have understood. But, according to the spiritual authority over my life that day, my great sin was singing about the goodness of God with my mother and father who loved Jesus.

The experience marked a turning point in my life. It fueled my anger and rebellion against religion. I was never angry at God but I raged against what I considered the abuse of a legalistic, merciless, and oppressive spiritual authority. **Romans 2:4 says that the goodness of God leads you to repentance.** Had I been taught more about God's love and less about the religious opinions of men, things would have been different. But as it was, I slid into a deep pit of despair.

Overwhelmed by the disappointment and the seeming impossibility of being a blessing and not a burden to my family, I put a gun to my head intending to commit suicide. I sat in my room for hours crying, praying, and trying to pull the trigger. Thank God, I'd heard enough of His Word to realize there is a heaven and a hell. The fear of spending eternity in hell saved my life that day.

At Left:
Graduation Day

At Right:
Working on a Song

GROWING UP IN EXILE

Walking down the hallway of yet another new school, I steeled myself against the stares of my new classmates and the scowls of the school bullies. Always the outsider, I felt like I was growing up in exile. My family traveled and moved so much that I attended 11 different schools before I graduated high school, three of them boarding schools. But in all of them, one thing remained the same: I didn't fit in and I knew it. My parents couldn't afford to buy me clothes that were in style. So I wore hand-me-downs from my brothers who were eight and nine years older than me. The clothes were so worn and outdated by the time I inherited them there was no way to hide it.

My appearance wasn't the only problem. I'd also begun to write songs—and the lyrics usually rhymed. I could hear the music in my head but the other boys in school thought I was writing poems. Let me just tell you, a boy who wrote poems in Georgia in the 1950s had to fight to prove his masculinity. Because I was so small, I made an easy target. In every new school I had to face down the bullies in a physical fight to prove they couldn't scare me. When I asked my father for help, he just told me to grab a stick or a brick and take them out in front of everybody. I learned that the quicker I did it, the better.

After fighting my way through my school days alone, I looked forward to holidays. But even they didn't ease my sense of isolation. Instead of bringing my family together, they were just another gig because we were always hired to sing for those special days of celebration.

When we moved to Philadelphia, I joined a Babe Ruth League baseball team. That year I had the highest batting average in Philly for a kid my age but my father never got to see one of my games. I loved my dad tremendously and longed for his approval, but he was a hard, strict, busy man. He never allowed me to get very close to him. He never had time to sit in the stands and cheer me on. In my life as at my baseball games, I continually looked for him and found him missing. Every time it happened, my anger mounted. His absence fanned the flames of my resentments, fears, and insecurities, and turned them into a rebellious rage that only Jesus could deliver me from.

FORGIVENESS

In the hospital right before he went to heaven, my dad and I asked each other for forgiveness. The restoration of a loving relationship between us opened the door for a change in me. A week after my dad died in 1980, I attended a Christian concert and gave my life to the Lord. I was 35 years old.

After I accepted the lordship of Jesus Christ, I went to my sweet momma and asked her to forgive me for the way my rebellion had affected her life. She forgave me and asked me to forgive her for not being there for me. We discussed it many times and I now understand the tough situation she faced during that difficult time of our lives: She was overwhelmed with the responsibility of being a wife, mother of five, and a TV personality who lived on the road. As the voice of the group, lead singer, and piano player, she carried the success of the group on her shoulders.

For me and for all of us, Momma had done the best she could. In the years before she was promoted to heaven, she and I really learned to enjoy each other. The Lord completely restored our relationship with mutual love and respect.

It could have never happened without Him.

If reading this has brought back memories of similar situations in your life, my prayer is that you will forgive all those who hurt you and allow God to heal you of any past hurts and restore you to a right relationship with Him and your family.

CHAPTER FIVE

HOW ELVIS CHANGED IT ALL

WITHOUT HIM

Without Him I could do nothing
Without Him I'd surely fail
Without Him, I would be drifting
Like a ship without a sail

Without Him I would be dying
Without Him I'd be enslaved
Without Him my life would be hopeless
But with Jesus, thank God I'm saved

Jesus, Oh Jesus
Do you know Him today
Please don't turn Him away
Oh Jesus, Precious Jesus
Without Him, how lost I would be

But with Jesus thank God I'm free

Lyrics by Mylon Le Fevre
Angel Band Music
Used by permission

On a clammy night in October 1962, I almost made the biggest mistake of my life. I almost gave up on getting to Memphis. Only 24 hours away from shaking the hand of the biggest star in the world and hearing the offer that would change everything for me, I was about to sling my duffel bag over my shoulder and head back to the barracks.

After all, I didn't know what was about to happen.

All I knew was that I'd trudged about 20 miles along a two-lane road in the freezing rain trying—and failing—to hitch a ride. I'd already wasted hours of my weekend pass. With 600 miles and the Smoky Mountains stretched between me and Memphis, I didn't see how I could make it there and still get back to the base by Monday morning. It looked impossible.

Shoulders sagging, with raindrops drizzling past my collar and down my neck, I thought about my family. I missed them so much. I hadn't seen them since I'd graduated from Reserve Training and gone active in the U.S. Army. (Getting drafted was inevitable in those days, so I'd decided at 17 years old to go ahead and join up— mostly because I wanted to get shaving my head over with. One of my life's goals back then was to grow a couple feet of hair. It's cool now to shave your head but in those days, I thought it was just plain rude!)

I'd started boot camp on June 12 and was stationed at Fort Jackson, South Carolina. The only contact I'd had with my family was by phone. So that week when I'd called my mom and she asked if I could come to Memphis for the weekend, I was eager to go. She wanted me to join the family at the Gospel Quartet Convention to sing my new song, "Without Him." I'd written it the previous year as a senior in high school while living in Fresno, California, with my sister Andrea and her husband Rev. Jerry Goff.

Andrea has moved on to heaven now, but she was always a sweet and kind sister to me. She tried to encourage and care for me in the areas where she knew Mom and Dad couldn't because of their traveling schedule. During my time at Andrea's, I'd really tried to learn more about God, and "Without Him" carried special meaning for me. I was eager to sing it at the convention. But, as I explained to Mom, you can't just take off for the weekend when you're in the Army; you have to have a weekend pass.

So I went to work figuring out how to get one.

It was widely known in our company that a bottle of Jack Black (Jack Daniels Black Label Whiskey) could be very persuasive, so I bought a pint for my staff sergeant. He granted me the pass and released me from my work detail about 5 p.m. on Friday evening. With no car and no money for a bus ticket, my plan was to walk to the base entrance before sundown because they didn't allow hitchhiking on the base, and thumb a ride from there.

I headed out with high hopes, but by 8:00 that night with cars whizzing past me like I was invisible, I was tired, hungry, frustrated, and desperate. My plan hadn't worked out as expected. Part of why I joined the Army was to become independent and establish my manhood, especially in the eyes of my dad. But here I was, soaking wet, standing in the pitch dark on a country road in the middle of nowhere; just a lonely teenager with tears in his eyes, frantic to reach his family. Obviously, being a man would have to wait. What I needed at that moment was a miracle.

All my life I'd heard that everything is possible with God. So, as I had so many times before, I stopped my world again and asked God for help. The next set of headlights coming toward me turned out to be my first of about 20 rides that weekend. Boy, I was glad to get in a warm, dry car!

After walking and hitchhiking all night and all day, I arrived in Memphis about 7:30 Saturday night. I didn't know where Ellis Auditorium was, but my last ride was a local guy who took me all the way to the backstage entrance. I arrived literally moments before my parents were scheduled to sing. God had miraculously made a way for me to show up for my divine appointment right on time.

ELVIS HAS NOT *LEFT THE BUILDING*

With no chance to shower, shave, or change clothes, I stepped onto the stage in my wrinkled, wet Army greens. I hadn't slept since 5:30 Friday morning and I'm sure I looked pretty worn out. When my mom introduced me to the audience, she explained what I'd gone through to get there. In those days, serving your country as a soldier was considered a great honor (I believe it still is) so the audience responded warmly to me.

As I began to sing my song, what I now know is the anointing power and presence of God came upon me. It was so strong it amazed me.

No one in the auditorium had any idea that Elvis Presley was listening to the concert that night. He'd come unannounced with his girlfriend, Priscilla, his producer, and his bodyguards (the Memphis Mafia) to pick out songs for the upcoming Gospel album he was about to record. Sitting in the booth that his manager, Colonel Tom Parker, had built to the side of the stage and equipped with one-way mirrors and recording equipment, Elvis could see out, but no one could see in.

Because he had just gotten out of the Army, the sight of me in my Army greens touched his heart. God gave me favor with him and he told the Colonel to bring me back to meet him.

When I walked into the side room, I was astonished to see Elvis Presley stand to shake my hand. He told me he really liked my singing and he wanted to record my song on his next gospel album, *How Great Thou Art*. I cannot describe what that did for my self-esteem.

I found out later that he told Colonel Tom not to take my publishing rights or copyrights, which was always standard practice when Elvis recorded somebody's song. I was a young kid and I knew nothing about the significance of publishing rights and copyrights. But because of that generous choice, "Without Him" is still blessing me financially today.

CRUISING IN HIGH COTTON

When Elvis recorded my song, he was the biggest star in the world. His album, *How Great Thou Art,* sold millions of copies and became his biggest seller up to that time, far surpassing his rock and roll recordings. The album instantly launched me into a realm of success that left me reeling. For the first time in my life people were acknowledging me as a songwriter.

The first royalty check I received put me in shock! I rode to the bank on my bicycle to cash it. (I didn't own a car.) When I handed it to the teller, she just stared—first at the check, then at me. Finally, she went over to the manager's office and said, "There's a kid out here wanting to cash this really big check from Elvis Presley."

I had no bank account because I'd never had enough money to open one. So the manager told me I'd have to wait for the bank in Memphis to verify the check. Then they'd need to request a special shipment of cash from the Federal Depository because they didn't keep that many big bills in their safe.

As a private in the Army, my paycheck totaled a whopping $84 a month. The only place I could afford to shop was the PX at Fort Jackson. But things were about to change! From Monday until Thursday while I was waiting for the royalty check to clear, I hit the stores and made a list of what I wanted to buy. My parents had done the best they could to provide for us kids but this was the first time in my life I could get exactly what I wanted instead of just what I needed. Man, I was in some high cotton!

A buddy of mine gave me a ride to the bank on Thursday to get my money. I had no briefcase, so I piled it in a Kroger grocery sack. What a sight to see that brown paper bag with all those hundred dollar bills in it!

I went as fast as I could to Central Chevrolet. When the salesman at the dealership first saw me, he wouldn't even talk to me. I was obviously just a skinny, poor kid dreaming of owning a sports car someday. What he didn't know was that was my day! By the time I left the dealership I was the happy owner of a brand-new 427 cubic inch Chevy Corvette with big, loud, chrome exhaust pipes and four in the floor. (That car only cost $5700. Can you believe it?)

At Right: "Without Him" *sheet music cover*
Upper Right: An old friend whose kindness helped me buy my first Corvette!

In short order, I purchased everything I ever dreamed of. My loot included a new Harley Davidson motorcycle, a Martin guitar, two pairs of Levi jeans, and a pair of leather Converse All Stars. I thought I was King Kong! Next, I rented an apartment at one of those fancy apartment complexes with a swimming pool and tennis courts. Other than a sound system and a TV, I wasn't interested in things like couches, lamps, and furniture. So for the first few months I just parked my Harley in the living room and slept on the floor beside it in my sleeping bag.

After Elvis recorded my song, I suddenly went from being the class joke to the most popular kid on the block. The king of rock and roll had given me some street credibility. Instead of getting pushed around and teased for writing what my classmates thought were poems, I started getting some respect. The guys who used to bully and make fun of me were saying to their friends, "Hey, there's my buddy Mylon. He writes songs for Elvis."

Of course, some of that respect might have been generated by the physical changes in me. When I'd joined the Army in the spring of 1963, my 201 file recorded my height at 5'4" and my weight at 120 pounds. Six months later, I'd grown 7 inches and gained 35 pounds of pure muscle. I used that muscle to put a few former bullies in their place. It was awesome.

There was just one downside. While the uniforms of the other soldiers faded over time from the original bright green that identified them as grunts or new recruits to duller color that proved seniority, my uniforms stayed bright green. Just when they'd start to fade the Army issued me new ones in bigger sizes. So I looked like a perpetual grunt.

In every other way, though, my social life improved dramatically. I didn't get many dates when my only means of transportation was a bicycle. But cruising around the hood flushed out in my new Corvette, I attracted the attention of girls who wouldn't even talk to me in school.

PUSHING THE ENVELOPE

After my hitch in the Army, I moved to Memphis, Tennessee. There, I joined J.D. Sumner and The Stamps Quartet, a group that eventually became the back-up group for Elvis until his death. Working with The Stamps

as a vocalist, songwriter, and bass player helped give me the essential self confidence a musician needs to be a leader in the studio and on stage. It was liberating for me creatively to have an influence in the direction of the musical genre I had grown up with.

On the other hand, I backslid spiritually as I became more obsessed with making it as a musician. I was singing about Jesus every day, but I don't think I would have recognized Him if He had gotten on our bus!

In addition to performing with The Stamps, I also sang for my family off and on for about three years. By "off and on," I mean I got fired a lot. The reason was simple: I viewed my father's leadership as domineering and he viewed me as a musical rebel, always trying to push the envelope. He and my mom felt apprehensive about my desire to expand our sound and style to appeal to a younger generation.

The last time I rejoined the family, my dad had supposedly turned over the management of our group to my older brother. Pierce was a real visionary and had always been my hero. He loved me and I loved and respected him. When he asked me to come home, I immediately gave my notice to The Stamps and went back to Atlanta.

Eager to help my family and excited by the offer of legal and equal partnership in The Le Fevre's Incorporated—which, by then, included a recording studio, a record company and a publishing company as well as our coast-to-coast syndicated TV show, all under the very capable supervision of my other older brother, Meurice—I tried to make peace with my dad. It lasted about 18 months. Then the years of tension between us came to a head.

I thought I had finally earned the right to have a voice in the future of our family because the royalties from my songs had helped finance the growth of the family business. But Dad couldn't see it that way. As hard as I believe he tried, he just couldn't relinquish control.

He eventually fired me for the last time when I refused to cut my sideburns for an album-cover photo session! The funny thing is, a few years later he was sporting those same sideburns and he wore them until the day he went to heaven.

When Dad gave me my walking papers, I knew it was time for me to go out on my own. For years I had been writing songs that were too contemporary for my family's musical style and attitude. I didn't do it to offend them. I did it because when I listened to the music inside me, that's what I heard. For a songwriter, songs are very personal. I knew intimately what each one should sound and feel like.

I had to protect my songs. So, in 1969, I started my first band.

At Right: *Mylon with his first band, the nucleus of which later became the* Atlanta Rhythm Section

CHAPTER SIX

ROCK AND ROLL

TRYING TO BE FREE

You are not the only one who understands the blues
You are not the only one who's had to pay some dues
Cause this old world's been putting me down
Kicking my sound and pushing me around
And I'm only trying to be free

When I was young I told myself I didn't need my family
But as I grew I realized I only wanted them to need me
But this old world has been pushing me round
Kicking my sound and putting me down
And especially my family

So now I've played my game
I've sung my song And I am free
And if I have your attention, if I have your attention
Then I've played sufficiently

Lyrics by Mylon Le Fevre
Copyright 1969
Angel Band Music
Used by permission

A WILD RIDE

I still have trouble wrapping my mind around it: how, in three short years, I went from making music with my first band, *Mylon*, in a makeshift rehearsal studio in a vacant Baptist church, to laying down tracks in an English mansion with legends the likes of George Harrison and Ron Woods. I was so messed up back then, I'm amazed it was even possible. And I'm even more amazed God was able to get me through it alive.

One thing's for sure, it was a wild ride.

It started with my band's first album, *We Believe*, which we recorded in 1969. Rock and Roll Hall of Famer, Allen Toussaint, produced it for Cotillion Records at Le Fevre Sound Studios in Atlanta. As far as I know, it was the first album recorded for a major secular record label by a contemporary Christian rock band. With its release, I was on my way to becoming the independent man and musician I'd always wanted to be.

But at 25 years old, I was also trying to find the truth about God. I wanted to know: What's He like? What does He really want me to do?

As I looked for the answer everywhere but the Bible, I got more angry and confused. It seemed that everyone I asked about God told me what He didn't like and why I was going to hell for not obeying Him. They gave me more religious rules and regulations. Because I heard little about God's amazing love, unending mercy, and grace, I thought I'd never be able to please Him. So I decided I'd just be respectful to Him in my own way and hope He'd be merciful.

To be clear, I don't blame my family, the church, or even the devil for that decision. Ultimately, I was the one who chose the self-destructive life I lived. If I'd read the Word of God and trusted Him, my life would have been different. But I didn't trust anybody in those days.

GLAD TO BE STONED

I'd been smoking reefer since I was a teenager. Grateful for any escape from the depression I suffered, I was ecstatic about it from the beginning. I was actually deceived enough to believe that God had created it (along with other "herbs and spices") just to cheer me up. I didn't see anything wrong with staying loaded and giggling about silly stuff all the time.

I remember calling my parents the first time I got stoned and telling my mom, "You and Dad have to try this. It will really help our family lighten up and enjoy our lives more." Momma freaked out. I heard her tell my dad, "Mylon's become a dope fiend!" Dad got on the phone and read me the riot act for upsetting Momma. He was really hot about it and I was really glad I was stoned.

During those early years of rock and roll, marijuana, cocaine, psychedelics, and speed seemed to be available at every concert. So, crazy as it sounds now, my band and I got on board. Before every rehearsal, concert, and recording session, we got high together. Then we circled up, joined hands, and prayed for God to bless us with hit songs and records. We thought we were all Christians simply because we weren't atheists, Buddhists, or Muslims. Raised in the Bible belt where going to church was the politically correct thing to do, for most of us Christianity was a religious tradition rather than a relationship.

I can honestly say that through all those years of excessive and eventually self-destructive drug abuse, I always believed that Jesus Christ was the Son of God. I even put crosses on all of my stage clothes, guitars, albums, and band equipment. I knew a lot *about* Jesus from all the things that others had told me. The problem was, *I did not really know Him.*

HOLY SMOKE

In early 1970, just months after our first album was released, our band landed a gig that put us on the fast track: We opened at The Capitol Theatre in Port Chester, New York, for a band called *Mountain*. Their phenomenal leader and bass player, Felix Pappalardi, had produced a couple of the biggest albums in the world for Eric Clapton and *Cream*.

Felix and I soon became close friends. I signed with his management company and he produced my next album. He also convinced CBS Records to buy my Cotillion contract so I could be on the same label as *Mountain*.

We named the new band *Mylon and Holy Smoke*, and toured with *Mountain* constantly for the next year.

Once I signed a contract with Felix, his Uncle Vito made some connections for us. Powerful and famous, Uncle Vito was the kind of man who could make you a deal you couldn't refuse. (Well, you could refuse, but if you did, you might become "accident prone.") He made a call to Frank Barsalona at Premier Talent Agency and all of a sudden I went from no gigs to performing with bands like *The Who*, *Traffic*, Alvin Lee and *Ten Years After*, the *Grateful Dead*, the *Allman Brothers*, Little Richard, *Jethro Tull*, the *Atlanta Rhythm Section*, *Emerson, Lake, & Palmer*, *Yes*, *The Beach Boys*, Tina Turner, *Procol Harum*, *J. Geils Band*, and *Grand Funk Railroad*. You get the idea.

In those days of adrenalin-filled adventures, I discovered that most of my rock and roll heroes slept a lot less than I did. So I altered my schedule to keep up. At times, especially in the studio, I recorded for 10 to 12 hours. Then I went to the hotel to get some sleep and came back the next day to work some more.

At Right: *Mylon with his band, Holy Smoke*

One day while recording at the Record Plant in New York, I was invited to a session down the hall where Stephen Stills and his band *Manassas* were working on a song called "Love the One You're With." A friend introduced me to cocaine that night. It gave me so much energy that we recorded for three days nonstop. We took breaks only to eat a little or take a quick shower.

It was a very prolific season for me creatively. Since it seemed I could accomplish more with the use of cocaine, I made a very stoned and deceived decision. I decided that sleep was the enemy of man and that I wasn't going to waste anymore time sleeping than I had to. I bought a kilo of coke that night and began a decade of hopeless years of addiction.

Upper Left: 1972 Central Park concert in New York City

Lower Left & Right: 1977 Varner Bros. album covers

the next 10 years, I rode a roller coaster of sex, drugs, and rock and roll. I thought I was living the dream. ring and recording with the biggest stars in the world, I flew in private jets. I lived in mansions, penthouse es, and castles. When I wasn't being chauffeured in limousines, I was driving some of the fastest and most rious cars in the world: Rolls Royces, Ferraris, Lamborghinis, Porsches, and Mercedes.

life rushed past at a manic pace. I averaged more than 300 concerts a year in a different city every night. One we performed for five nights in a row, from Christmas until New Year's Eve, at Fillmore East in New York , but for the most part we did one night stands all over the world. The relentless touring, writing, recording never going home became more pressure than I could handle. Every night I went on stage and shared my ic and dreams with about 20,000 people. Sometimes, at festivals, over 100,000 showed up. They treated me he most part like a hero. But as soon as the show was over, we would get in the limo and go to the hotel. Eve gh we might be staying in the penthouse suite at the nicest hotel in town, the loneliness was overwhelming ss you took somebody back to the room with you.

n there was the fear. Horrible and totally unreasonable, it drove me without mercy. No matter how many ding ovations our band received in a row, I spent every night tormented by the terror that the next crowd ldn't like my music. Literally sick at my stomach with a fear of rejection that would haunt me for years, I tried et higher and higher before every gig.

scape my exhaustion, confusion and developing paranoia, I took every drug but birth control, and they were vailable in unlimited quantities. The more I bought and paid cash for, the purer the quality. I went from sing around with heroin to numb the loneliness and desperation, to total addiction.

n addict, my lifestyle was to get wired up on coke or meth for the concert and stay up all night. But heroin my drug of choice. Once, in Paris, France, I scored some heroin that was a lot stronger than I was used to. I dosed and it was just the grace of God that kept me alive that night. I became conscious enough about dawn ll my mom in Atlanta and ask her to pray. I went unconscious again while she was praying but God had y on me that day. I tried going cold turkey a couple of times but never could stay clean. The depression was too great and the drugs too available. Desperate and knowing I had to do something, I decided I needed a change of friends and scenery.

Upper Right: *Filming* The Midnight Special *in London with Alvin Lee and Steve Winwood from* Traffic

Lower Left: *With Alvin*

Lower Right: *With Alvin and Wolfman Jack*

51

HAZY DAYS IN THE GLASS HOUSE

That Christmas, after three months of touring together, Alvin Lee invited me to join him in Jamaica for a vacation.

A world class guitar player, Alvin and his band, *Ten Years After*, had become internationally famous almost overnight because of the Woodstock festival and movie. He'd also become my best friend—not just because of his talent but because of his honesty. If Alvin gave you his word, you could take it to the bank, a rare thing in rock and roll. He smoked a lot of hash and reefer but he never got strung out on hard drugs. When we toured together, we'd hang out after the gig and jam and write songs. He had a great sense of humor and was a good influence on me.

Alvin had rented a getaway called the Glass House in St. Ann's Bay for the Christmas holidays. The place was ridiculous! Unless you pulled the curtains, you could see right through the house. Every room offered fabulous views. On the north side, you could see the lush mountain greenery, a rainbow of tropical flowers, and foliage interspersed with papaya, banana and coconut trees. In the other direction was the pool, cabana and the beach. The water was so clear and the sand so white that you could stand on the boat dock and watch brightly colored fish darting around the shallow reef below.

Alvin and I spent the next three weeks just chilling, snorkeling, horseback riding on the beach, and smoking Jamaican mountain ganja. We jammed with the local reggae band, wrote songs and talked about doing an album together some day. We also went to the local theatre in town a couple of times to watch movies. One night a tropical storm blew in torrential rains. That's when we discovered the architecturally beautiful, new theatre building didn't have a roof. We'd been sitting under the stars without knowing it. Dude, that was some serious ganja!

The owner of the house we rented had stocked the library with some really good books. One of them, a weird book called the *Guinness Book of World Records*, documented all kinds of crazy things people had done to set or break a record. One night after supper while under the influence of some local herbs, Alvin and I decided to get our names added to the list. We discussed our greatest areas of expertise and decided to roll and smoke the world's largest joint.

The rules in the book were very specific. Everything you did had to be measured, weighed, photographed, witnessed, and documented. (I had forgotten all about this until recently when I told Alvin I was writing a book and asked him to send me some pictures. He said that reminded him of our Guinness project and emailed me some of our official documentation.) The joint, Mr. Doobie as we referred to it, was 28 ½ inches long and 1 ½ inches in diameter. It took us three hours and 42 minutes to smoke it. I'm sure you'll forgive me if I don't remember exactly what it weighed. A lot of things were sort of hazy that day—including the Polaroid pictures we took of each other every 15 minutes. They got more out of focus with each shot. The last few showed nothing but the ceiling!

The next day while trying to get the required witnesses to sign and notarize our documentation, it was brought to our attention by Alvin's manager that what we were referring to as *documentation* might be viewed as *evidence* by certain agencies of the government. Needless to say, we did not get in the *Guinness Book of World Records*

YOU CAN'T JUST INVITE A BEATLE TO YOUR HOUSE.

I'd already been busted for dope several times in the United States. The next bust could possibly include incarceration. So after my vacation in Jamaica, I figured I should change my routine. Instead of going to New York City after my next tour like I usually did, where I'd be around musicians who weren't the best influence for a guy wanting to get clean, I decided I'd head for England.

Once again, Alvin extended an invitation to spend some time at his castle in the English countryside and enjoy some fresh scenery while I was detoxing. We also decided to record some of the songs we had written together.

When I told him I was going to take him up on his offer, he started building a beautiful state-of-the-art recording studio in what had been horse stables at his magnificent, fourteenth century estate. It was a wonderful change for me at the time. I'm a country boy at heart and the acres of wheat fields dancing in the breeze at springtime were truly therapeutic to me. Alvin and I would always ride a couple of my Harley Davidson motorcycles when he visited me in Atlanta, so he bought some really cool dirt bikes. We rode until the sun went down more than once. I loved it. I'd had enough of downtown hotels in big cities for a while. The streets of New York were pretty intimidating for a country boy from Georgia.

While we were writing more songs for the album, I started calling some English buddies I had met on tour back in the States. Of course, when they came over to hang out we did what musicians always do, we jammed. A few songs were really coming together, so we decided to lay down some tracks. Roger Daltrey, the lead singer of *The Who*, let us use his private recording studio at his castle until Alvin got the new one finished.

On the early tracks, Alvin played lead guitar, and Boz Burrell from the band *Bad Company* played bass. Ian Wallace from *King Crimson* and Jim Capaldi from *Traffic* took turns sitting in on drums. The keyboards on the early sessions were played by Tim Hinkley, a renowned session man from London. He was eventually joined by Steve Winwood from *Traffic* as soon as his tour was over.

Steve called in Rebop, *Traffic's* percussionist all the way from Trinidad. His syncopation on congas and timbales really helped solidify the rhythm section. I usually sang and played a little acoustic guitar or bass or percussion if it was needed. As word got out about the sessions, Ronnie Woods came in and helped us write and played some smoking slide guitar. Woody had recently left Rod Stewart's band to join *The Rolling Stones* but the *Stones* weren't touring at that time.

One day we drove over to the beautiful little village of Henley on the Thames. We went there to eat some Shepherd's Pie and drink a few pints of Exhibition Ale at a quaint little place on the river called the Angel Pub. While we were waiting on our food, George Harrison and a couple of friends came in and sat down at the table next to us. I told Alvin I was going to ask George if he wanted to come over and jam with us that night. Alvin got real serious and very English. His voice quiet but intense, he said to me, "Don't even think about it! You can't just invite a Beatle over to your house."

I said, "I can."

Before Alvin could protest any more, I leaned over and introduced myself to George. He was very friendly and gracious. I explained that I was a gospel rocker from Georgia and that my friends and I were making a record at a really relaxed pace just a few kilometers down the road. Then I told him he was welcome to come over and hang out and jam a little if he wanted. Alvin was trying to act like he didn't know me.

ON THE ROAD TO FREEDOM

George and I became really good friends after that. He was in the middle of his first award-winning solo album, *All Things Must Pass,* and he'd just built a new studio at his home, Friar Park, a former monastery on some beautiful acreage outside Henley. When he found out that Alvin's studio wasn't quite finished yet, he invited us to use his as long as we needed.

Because all of the guys were still in very successful bands, sometimes somebody would be missing when we wanted to lay down a track. One night when both of our drummers were on tour I asked George if he knew a good drummer we could get for a session. He said his brother-in-law was a good drummer and that he would bring him to the session that night. When I told Alvin, he panicked. "Uh-oh, dude! What if his brother-in-law is a lousy drummer?"

ROCKIN TIL THE SUN GOES DOWN

I've been to Liverpool
Been to Birmingham
Been to New Orleans
Honey, Been Around

Rocking is the reason
I go town to town
And I will still be rocking
When the sun goes down

I'm gonna' keep on rocking
until the sun goes down...

Lyrics by Alvin Lee and
Mylon Le Fevre
Chrys-a-lee Music/
Holy Smoke Music
Used by Permission

At Right: "On the Road to Freedom" *Album Cover with Alvin Lee*

That night we found out George Harrison and Mick Fleetwood from the band Fleetwood Mac had married sisters. George's brother-in-law was a monster drummer.

After Alvin and George became good friends, we were relaxing in the studio one night after a session and I asked George why he had agreed to play on our album when he'd never played on anybody else's but the Beatles. George just put his hand on my shoulder, looked me right in the eye and said "Mylon, you were the first person who ever invited me." You should have seen the smile on Alvin's face.

That same summer, I got a call from Pete Townsend, the legendary lead guitar player/songwriter for the band *The Who*. He had just written a rock opera called *Tommy* and was making it into a movie. He asked me to arrange and sing some background vocals for the movie soundtrack. It was a blast. I really enjoyed that project. I also invited Pete to play on our album. He wanted to, but he was under a deadline to finish mixing his own project in time for the movie release.

Strange as it seems, Alvin's driveway became the symbol of that wonderful year of music making. A long and winding road that threaded through miles of beautiful forest around his estate, led to the Manor House where we were hidden from the chaos of touring, airports, security, and hotels. So we called it, "The Road to Freedom." Over the next year we recorded the album that we created there and named it by the same name.

On the Road to Freedom was released in America in 1973 on CBS Records.

THE MIDNIGHT SPECIAL

As soon as the label released the first single, they wanted us to start touring and promoting the album immediately. It was so exciting! The English press referred to our band as "a Super Group." We taped our first public gig, a TV show called "The Midnight Special," at the Rainbow Room on the top floor of Biba's Department Store in London. Steve Winwood got a release from his record company but George Harrison was in litigation with his label and they wouldn't release him. So we set up his amps and microphone off camera. You could hear him but you couldn't see him. In fact, when the record was released we credited George as Hari Georgeson for legal reasons and because of his spiritual beliefs in Hare Krishna.

backstage

Upper Right: 1976 *With Pete Townsend of* The Who

Lower Left: *On tour with Mick Fleetwood of* Fleetwood Mac

Lower Right: 1978 *With Tina Turner on tour*

Opposite Page:

Upper Left: 1970 *With Little Richard in the studio, Miami*

Upper Right: *With Eric Clapton, New York City*

Lower Left: *With Greg Allman of the* Allman Brothers

Lower Right: *With Steve Winwood and Alvin Lee on*

Upper Left: *1971-Mylon's producer & manager Felix Pappalardi. Toured together with Felix's band,* Mountain

Upper Right: *1977- With Willie Nelson backstage at Charlie Daniels' Volunteer Jam*

Lower Left: *With Charlie Daniels*

Lower Right: *With then President Jimmy Carter and a member of the Outlaws*

On the Road to Freedom was a musical phenomenon for one simple reason: It was literally free. That's why so many famous musicians wanted to be a part of it. Most of us were already millionaires. Making good music and having fun was our only motive. So, for the first time, we financed the project ourselves. We used Alvin's studio for most of the recording/mixing and everybody played for free.

When you don't take the record company's money then they can't constantly put pressure on you to meet deadlines and record songs where they own the publishing rights, et cetera. It was the most relaxed project I'd been a part of since I was a teenager. We were just making music because we loved to feel and hear it.

On the other hand, the very thing that made the album so wonderful doomed it from the start. The managers and especially the record company executives, intimidated by the thought of musicians being in control of the system, felt like the inmates were running the asylum! They released the record and it sold really well but they refused to spend the money to promote it properly in the U.S. So, of course, it slowly rode off into the sunset. All the musicians went back to their bands. And it was over.

Everyone was disappointed but I was devastated. The world tour I'd dreamed of my whole life, with my best friends and rock and roll's best musicians, had been canceled. I went home to Georgia, a failure in my own eyes. I wanted to come home a hero to my family, especially to my little girl, Summer.

But that painful disappointment drove me deeper into the manic depression I had fought my whole life. I kept recording and touring but fell back into a dependency on an endless cycle of drug induced highs and lows.

Some 25 years later George Harrison finally did what he had said he would. He got Bob Dylan, Tom Petty, Roy Orbison, and Jeff Lynne together and pulled off the dream. They called themselves *The Traveling Wilburys*.

*I'm just a poor boy from
down in Georgia
But I'm riding on a big jet plane
I don't know what I'm doing here
But I guess I can't complain
I'm just flying around the country
And I'm banging on my guitar
And I'm telling everybody
who will listen to me
I'm gonna' be a big
Rock and Roll star*

Lyrics by Mylon Le Fevre
Angel Band Music
Used by permission

At Right: 1972- *With George
Harrison in the studio*
Lower Left: *One of George's
homes, Friar Park, where I stayed
and recorded*
Lower Right: *With Ron Woods of
The Rolling Stones and Alvin Lee
of Ten Years After in the studio at*

CHAPTER SEVEN

BRAND NEW START

BRAND NEW START

I cannot take it, I cannot make it
I will not fake it again
I been so tired, Of being so wired
And not ever fired-up within

Here is my guitar
My rock and roll star
It wasn't really that far-out
So Lord help me be true
I just wanna love you
So teach me to trust you without doubt

I just need revival in my soul
Won't you please come and take control
And send your spirit to my heart
And give my life a brand new start

Lyrics by Mylon Le Fevre
Angel Band Music/Dayspring Music
Used by permission

After the demise of the "On the Road to Freedom" tour, I returned home to Atlanta to search for relief from the torment and depression that plagued me. I needed help, but I was too lost to find it. So, God made a way for help to find me.

While I was out in California promoting the album with Alvin, I bumped into an old friend, Fletch Wiley, from Andrae' Crouch's band. He invited me to go with him to a church called The Church on the Way, pastored by Jack Hayford. During the service, I sat behind this big, tall guy with long hair who kept raising his hands to worship God. I found out after church that he was a record producer named Buck Herring.

Buck and his wife, Annie, recognized me from my first Christian rock album, *We Believe*. They invited me to their home for lunch and began the nine year process of leading me back to the Lord through their persistent, loving witness.

During those years, whenever I needed someone to talk to that I knew loved God but wouldn't judge me for my lifestyle, I always called Buck. He'd wake up from a deep sleep to take my calls in the middle of the night. He'd listen to my despair and every time point me to the love of Jesus. If Buck ever tired of me, he didn't let it show. He was always there for me.

In the late 1970s, he asked me to come to California to sing background vocals for a Phil Keaggy album titled *Love Broke Through.* We recorded in his garage, which had no air conditioning, so it was really hot. I was still addicted to Quaaludes (sleeping pills) and usually went to sleep around 3 or 4 a.m. Buck, determined to help me connect with Jesus, would wake me up every morning at 8. I was a zombie but he'd force-feed me exotic coffees and lead me in Bible study and prayer.

Although I was still stuck in my old ways, God really touched my heart during those days. I'll never forget how He filled that sweltering garage with His presence as I tried to sing "Love Broke Through" without crying.

THE NIGHT THE WALLS CRUMBLED

A couple of years after those recording sessions, Buck reached out to me again. He invited me to come see his family's group, the *2nd Chapter of Acts,* while they were performing in Atlanta. I sat in the back of the auditorium behind the sound booth. What I experienced completely changed my life!

Growing up I'd seen lots of people sing about Jesus, but that night I watched people who were in love with Him sing to Him. They seemed to be so comfortable in their intimacy with Him. They genuinely celebrated the Lord. As they did, His presence filled the auditorium.

The Bible says, *the love of God is what draws men to repentance.* I can testify that it's true. Even in my stoned stupor, God's love began to crumble the walls of defense I had built around my heart. As the evening progressed, I started to weep as I sensed His perfect peace all around me.

Finally, I found what I'd been looking for my whole life—the sweet, holy presence of God!

When the music ended, Buck stood up and closed the concert with exactly what I needed to hear. He explained that *there is a life-changing difference between knowing Jesus is the Son of God, and trusting Him and submitting to Him as your Lord and Master.* Realizing I'd never truly trusted God, I cried out to Him and asked Him to forgive me and help me. I said "Lord, I understand now that I have always tried to be the lord of my own life.

If it's not too late and You can do anything with my messed-up life, then I give it to You. Jesus, I receive You as my Lord and my Savior."

With those words, an immense heaviness lifted off my chest. I instantly knew that God had forgiven me and I could start my life over again.

THE SAME THING CAN HAPPEN TO YOU

If you are ready to give your life to the Lord, you can pray the same simple prayer that I did.

God is listening! Jesus is ready and willing to put His life inside you and make you a new person right now. All you need to do is say this to Him and really mean it:

Father God, I come to You in the Name of Your Son, Jesus, and I confess my need for Your mercy right now. Please forgive me for all my sins and fill me with Your Holy Spirit. I turn from my old way of living, and with Your help I will study Your Word and learn how to live for You. Jesus, I accept and confess You as my Lord and Savior. Thank You for living and dying for me. Thank You for giving me all the blessing You deserve and for taking upon Yourself the punishment that I deserve. Thank You for saving my life, Jesus. I give it to You now. Amen.

Glory to God! According to God's Word, if you prayed that prayer from your heart, you just became a joint heir with Jesus Christ! That means everything Jesus has inherited from God now belongs to you too. It also means you just became my brother or sister in the Lord, so please know that I'll be praying for you and believing God with you for His best.

Now that you've established your relationship with Jesus, be sure to get into a good, Spirit-filled, Bible-believing church that will teach you how to live by faith in God's Word. Get a good Bible that is easy to understand. (I suggest the New Living Translation.) And here's one last bit of advice: From this time forward, concentrate on paying more attention to the Word of God than anybody else's words. His Word is the truth, and He will show up and prove it for anyone who believes it and speaks it consistently!

SUNDAY MORNING

After the concert Saturday night, I told Buck that I'd asked the Lord to forgive me and help me start my life over. He said I needed to get involved in church right away because that was where I would meet my new family in the Lord.

I didn't understand this back then as solidly as I do now, but the fact is, we all need a church family. We need a safe place where we can get together with those of like precious faith and encourage each other in the Lord. We need the help God provides for us through the ministry gifts of apostles, prophets, evangelists, pastors, and teachers. That's why God commanded us to never forsake "the assembling of ourselves together" (Hebrews 10:25), especially as we get closer to the return of Jesus.

Eager to follow Buck's instructions, I stayed up all night so I wouldn't miss church the next day. But when I got there some of my new family didn't seem too thrilled to see me.

Because I didn't own any suits and ties, I was still wearing what I'd worn to the concert the night before—leather, feathers, and earrings. I arrived early and chose a seat on the front row. After a while, a lady walked in and stood in front of me, staring daggers. I could tell she was mad but I couldn't figure out why. I thought maybe she wasn't used to seeing a man with so much hair. Years later, I found out the way I looked was only half the problem. The other half was that I was sitting in her usual place. Clearly, she would have rather seen me lost in sin than in her seat at church.

But I didn't care what she thought, or anybody else for that matter. I was so thankful I wasn't going to hell anymore and I had more pressing things on my mind than seating arrangements: I had a major drug addiction to deal with.

AN ACT OF GOD

I'd tried to kick heroin by going cold turkey many times so I knew how terrible the withdrawal symptoms were. So I kept waiting for the cycle of sweating, nausea, stomach cramps, vomiting, and pain to begin. I sat in church terrified that I might start getting the shakes right in the middle of the service.

But those terrible results of the abuse I had put my body through never came. *When I gave my life to Jesus, He instantly delivered me from heroin and cocaine addiction.* My prayer for help hadn't included deliverance from drugs simply because I didn't know it was possible. But God had set me free anyway, and I was free indeed!

I knew I couldn't serve God and continue to hang around the drugs and groupies in rock and roll, so I asked my lawyer to get me out of all my contracts. He found a clause that stated I could be released from them in the instance of an "act of God." In the legal sense, an act of God usually refers to natural disasters like getting struck by lightning or drowning in a flood. But my lawyer came up with a new definition. He argued that my becoming a Christian was literally an act of God.

Ultimately, the powerful people who controlled my musical career from behind the scenes let me out of my contracts with one stipulation: I had to relinquish all the royalties from my songs, publishing, and recordings. It cost me a fortune but it was a small price to pay compared to what it cost Jesus to deliver me from eternity in hell.

THE HEAD OF THE HEAD

After getting over the shock of my first Sunday morning experience, I developed a wonderful relationship with the pastor of the church, Dr. Paul Walker. He already knew who I was because I'd come to him for help about five years earlier, at a time when I was really strung out. As he liked to remind me, I was the only person who ever smoked a joint in his car while he was trying to minister to me! A precious man of God, Dr. Walker, and his associate pastor, Dr. M.G. McLuhan, became instrumental in discipling me through those tough, early years of my walk with the Lord.

Because I'd been in the habit of sleeping all day and partying all night, one of my first challenges was turning my days and nights around. I explained to Dr. Walker that I needed something to do during the day because all my old friends were drug addicts and night people. He solved the problem by entrusting me with a new responsibility. He informed me that because of my previous leadership skills, he was promoting me to "head of the head." It was his way of saying he had given me the job of church janitor!

I can laugh about it now, but back then I felt humiliated. I thought because I had toured the world and made a lot of money, I was too important to be cleaning floors and toilets. But after wasting several months on that proud attitude, I changed my perspective. I decided to clean the Family Life Center just for Jesus. As soon as I willingly humbled myself, God promoted me into youth ministry. I just wish it hadn't taken me so long to get my attitude right!

I was so amazed about my new life that I started telling everybody about it and soon led some of my old musician friends to the Lord. I also met some new friends who were musicians at a Bible study I was attending. In our free time we started doing what all musicians do: jamming. But this time we did it in a whole new way. We not only played music, we fasted, prayed, and studied God's Word together. Over time, our little jam sessions/prayer times produced what would later become the Christian rock band, *Mylon and Broken Heart*.

Dr. Walker did his part to help us along. He wisely allowed several of the musicians who had committed their lives to the Lord to become church janitors also. They all learned some valuable lessons pushing lawn mowers, mops, and brooms, and the ex-rockers/janitors club soon became a very powerful ministry called Broken Heart Ministries.

CHAPTER EIGHT

MYLON AND BROKEN HEART

MORE

Touch my heart and change my mind
Cut me loose from ties that bind
Lead me as I follow you
Give me strength to follow through
More, More, I wanna be more like Jesus

More of Jesus, less of me
By His power I will be
Like a flower in the spring
Brand new life in everything

Holy Spirit, fill me up
Gently overflow my cup
Touch my eyes and let me see
Me in you and you in me
More, More, I want to be more like Jesus

Lyrics by Mylon Le Fevre
Angel Band Music
Used by permission

What started as a simple musical outlet turned into a worldwide ministry. Young people, drawn to our concerts by rock and roll, heard the gospel and gave their lives to Jesus. Hard-edged kids who'd been turned off by religion got turned on to God. We thought it was awesome.

But not everybody was as happy about it as we were. Some folks were downright upset.

Many Church leaders weren't yet convinced you could rock and still be a Christian. Church bands were unheard of back then. They would have tarred and feathered us if we'd played our drums and electric guitars in a Sunday morning service. Some ministries even believed they were called by God to find fault with our style of music. Well meaning Christians spent hundreds of hours listening to our records backward, trying to find something evil in them.

To be fair, they didn't limit their investigations to us. They also reversed songs on albums like *Her Satanic Majesty's Request* by *The Rolling Stones*, or *Highway to Hell* by *AC/DC*. Then they produced videos about the bad things they thought they heard. What always amazed me was that you could hear more evil stuff playing those albums forward than they thought they heard playing them backward!

Although our only purpose as a band was to bless people and glorify God, well known Christian leaders persecuted us. They claimed on national TV that we were either homosexuals (because of our long hair) or demon possessed (because we were playing rock and roll and using smoke, lights, and pyrotechnics). A few didn't go quite that far. They just believed we were having too much fun; therefore we couldn't possibly be anointed!

But despite all the faultfinders, God opened doors for us that no man could close.

In just the first year of services in the church gym and around the city of Atlanta, we led almost 1800 young people to the Lord. My pastor instructed me not to try to disciple the kids at our concerts because we had all just been born again and we didn't know how. Our minds were still being renewed from all the drugs. Our job was to testify, lead them to Jesus, and invite them to church, where they could be discipled.

Some of the kids we led to the Lord were drug addicts, living on the streets as runaways or prostitutes. Some were hippies wearing love beads and tie-dyed shirts. Some were punkers with black fingernails, torn clothes, and a Goth lifestyle. Some had blue or green Mohawk haircuts and some were tobacco-chewing, beer-guzzling, redneck brawlers. They came in every race and color, but they all had one thing in common: They were all sinners who needed Jesus. They were just what we had been praying for!

But because they didn't look like typical Bible-belt church members, they weren't readily accepted into mainstream churches. (These days many ministries reach out to the misunderstood people living beyond the fringes of society, and I thank God for them. But back then, those people were not welcome in most churches.) Many of the kids we reached came to church with habits and appearances that intimidated not only people in the congregation, but deacons, elders, and board members as well.

One group of leaders in our church actually petitioned Dr. Walker to stop us from holding concerts in the church gym. Threatening to withdraw their financial support, they demanded that he "ban the sinners."

I was so proud of my pastor's response! He called a meeting, stood up, and bluntly said, "We are the Church of Jesus Christ. This is not your church or mine. If we ever discourage sinners from coming to church, we'll be nothing more than a religious country club. And if you continue with this, I will resign." The Word of God says that Jesus came for those living in darkness because they don't know the truth. All of us who belong to Him are instructed to go into **all** the world, to **all** people (no matter their race, profession, culture, sexual orientation, or financial status) and teach and preach and make disciples. So, with Dr. Walker still at the helm, that's what our congregation decided to do.

With the dispute settled in our home church, our band was off and running! God promoted us over the next 15 years and we eventually headlined almost every major contemporary Christian festival in the world. Blessed by the Lord with the funds to keep expanding, our ministry built a 24,000 square foot office/warehouse facility. It had a recording studio, a small gym/racquetball/volleyball court, a garage for our double-decker tour bus and 18-wheeler, an electrical and mechanical shop, 25 offices, and a 200-seat meeting room for our weekly Bible studies.

MY HEART BELONGS TO HIM

My mind has been a battlefield, where
many wars were fought
My soul has been a marketplace where
others sold and bought
But through the lonely wasted years
There's One who knew my hidden fears
And noticed the unnoticed tears
Now my heart belongs to Him

I gave my heart to Jesus
Because He set me free from sin
And that's just how He frees us
When we really let Him in
So I welcome all the changes
That His holiness arranges
Cause my heart belongs to Him

No one's ever touched my heart, the way that Jesus did
No one knew the place to start to find the pain I'd hid
But love can see where friends are blind
When lovers leave, love stays behind
But God is love, and His love is mine
Now my heart belongs to Him

Lyrics by Mylon Le Fevre
And Bill Morris
Angel Band Music
Used by permission

*1987 **Grammy** for "Crack the Sky"*
Best Gospel Performance

We also won a Grammy and four Dove awards. I'm extremely honored that many of the successful Christian rock musicians and music historians today accredit our band as one of the forerunners who paved the way for the praise and worship music the Church enjoys today. But I'm most thankful for the opportunity God gave us during those fruitful years to lead more than 200,000 young people to the lordship of Jesus Christ. What a holy privilege to play a part in helping hurting people find their place in the kingdom of God!

A BROKEN HEART

In August 1989, it all came to a screeching halt. Thirty-plus years of traveling millions of miles by plane, bus, and car, along with all the years of abuse I'd inflicted on my body, finally caught up with me. On the way to a concert in Lincoln, Nebraska, I suffered a heart attack in the back of our tour bus while talking to a couple of the guys in the band.

It hurt so bad, it temporarily paralyzed me. I couldn't breathe and I couldn't even move enough to tell my friends what was happening. The doctors later informed me that about a third of my heart had ceased to function properly. On the CAT scan, the area appeared black which meant there was no blood flow, heat, or life there. The experts explained to me that the heart is just a muscle and it cannot regenerate itself. The good news, according to the doctors, was that I could continue living with only two-thirds of my heart working. But I would have to get off the road completely, go home, and just sit and take it easy.

I knew that wasn't the way God wanted me to live. What the doctors described to me was survival. It was not the abundant life in Christ God promised in His Word. As a child attending tent meetings with my parents, I'd seen many people receive miracles of healing. I'd watched God do for them what the doctors couldn't. Now it was my turn.

At Right: On stage at the Dove Awards with Russ Taff, Imperials, Amy Grant & Michael W. Smith

THE WARRIOR

Many years on the road
Many more miles to go
We cannot waste another single day
The nights are hard and long
But He has made us strong enough
To take His love and give it all away
And I know—He said to go

Cause there's a war that's going on
a soul is raging
A battle weary warrior's somewhere praying
And you must understand
what the song is saying
Come on home to the Father
Come on home to the Son
Come on home the battles over, Christ has won

Tonight could be the night
You could see the light
And you could trade your worst in for His best
And He could take your sin
And cast it in the wind
As far as from the east into the west
And I know it's almost time to go

Lyrics by Mylon Le Fevre
Angel Band Music/Dayspring Music
Used by permission

CREATION FESTIVAL 1987
Broken Heart *headlined most of the major
Christian music festivals in the world*

83

ON THE ROAD AGAIN
Shooting videos and album covers from Key West to San Francisco

BROKEN HEART TOURING BUS & TRUCK

What a blessing this German double-decker bus and truck were for our band. At the time, the bus, semi-truck, and 40,000 pounds of sound and lighting gear were the best money could buy!

CHAPTER NINE

THE CALL

INVINCIBLE LOVE

I looked across the great divide
To a place called healed
I needed to reach the other side
When I saw the truth revealed. Then I crossed the
line. And saw the glory of His words replacing
mine. Just in time, His

Invincible love was all that could save me
Invincible love was the love that He gave me
Invincible love, coming down from above
Invincible love

Who is the healer of my heart
The Lord strong and able
My enemies watched me from the start
As He prepared me a table
And as I dine, He serves the fruit of peace
And the power of new wine
As a sign of

Invincible love was all that could save me
Invincible love was the love that He gave me
Invincible love, coming down from above
Invincible love

Lyrics by Scott Allen and Mylon Le Fevre
Angel Band Music
Used by permission

ANOTHER DIVINE APPOINTMENT

Desperate to get quiet so I could pray for direction and hear from God, I asked my brother, Meurice, if I could stay at his condo on the beach in Florida for a few weeks. There, I started reading a book entitled *Healing the Sick* by T.L. Osborne. The scriptures I found in it stirred hope within me for a miracle.

Although I didn't know it, Kenneth and Gloria Copeland were preparing to minister at a church about a mile away. They also happened to be staying at the same resort. On my third morning of fasting, I was walking down the beach praying in the Spirit and I passed in front of Gloria and her mom. (Talk about a divine appointment!) They were sitting in the sun reading their Bibles. When Gloria glanced up and saw me, the Spirit of the Lord spoke to her and told her I was in serious need of healing.

Enjoying a much needed day off, she wasn't looking for anybody to minister to—especially some guy in a swimsuit with a couple of feet of hair! But when she returned to the condo, she told Kenneth about me. He said, "Well, we just need to agree according to Matthew 18:19." Then he prayed "Father, Gloria and I touch and agree regarding this request. We ask You to bring this man to us and we will obey Your instructions to minister healing to him. In Jesus Name, Amen." His prayer was very simple but full of faith and power.

The next day I went to the pool with my Bible to get some sun and read and pray. Kenneth and Gloria, back from their morning service, were having lunch in their condo. When they stepped out on their balcony to take in the view, Gloria looked down at the pool and saw me. "Kenneth," she said, "there's that guy I told you about."

They pointed me out to the pastor who was hosting the services and he said, "Oh, I know him. He and his band *Broken Heart* came here 10 years ago to do a spring-break outreach for me in the early days of my church." Little did I know when I sowed that seed of service a decade earlier, it would one day be instrumental in me receiving my miracle. It still blesses me to think about how the divine hand of God moved so perfectly orchestrating my answer to prayer!

A BROKEN HEART MADE WHOLE

When I met the Copelands, Kenneth repeated to me what the Lord had spoken to Gloria. Then he shook my hand and said with a really big smile on his face, "You don't know my wife, but she doesn't play church. If she said God told her He's going to heal you, it's a done deal. So get ready to be healed."

The presence of God was so strong on this man; I didn't know what to do. I just stood there and cried.

Brother Copeland invited me into his condo and made me feel right at home. As we hung out that night, I was amazed at how peaceful, humble, and down to earth this wonderful couple was. Sitting down with his Bible, Kenneth proceeded to teach me about faith and healing. We spent hours talking and reading God's Word. We read everything Jesus said and did when He worked the 19 healing miracles recorded in Matthew, Mark, Luke, and John.

Kenneth told me God loved me and wanted to heal me. He explained that anybody can have mountain moving faith if they want it bad enough. It just takes time. Quoting Romans 10:17, he reminded me, "Faith comes by hearing and hearing by the Word of God. So the more Word you hear in your heart, the more your faith will grow strong!"

I already knew God *could* heal me *if* it was His will. But that night I learned *it is always God's will to save, heal, deliver, anoint, and bless His children.* I'll never forget Kenneth's words. "Son, you don't have to talk God into being good. He's good whether anybody likes it or not. And He is always doing good things for whoever truly believes Him and receives from Him. For the Lord is good and His mercy endures forever."

Sure enough, God had mercy on me that night and gave me a new heart!

I didn't need a lightning bolt from heaven to know it, either. As we'd studied the scriptures, I'd realized that whatever I believed would be done for me. So when Kenneth showed me in Mark 11:22-24 that I must believe I receive my miracle *when I pray*, and not when I feel the symptoms disappear from my body, the revelation hit me.

I knew exactly what to do. "Lay hands on me, Brother Copeland," I said. "I'm ready to receive my healing from God."

In the natural realm, nothing changed. I felt no different. In fact, the symptoms persisted for ten and a half months. Some nights I would be on stage doing moves with the band under the heat of hundreds of thousands of watts of lighting, and my chest would start hurting again. It felt like I was going to have another heart attack. But I'd just stop and testify about my faith in God, His Word, and His healing power working in my body. Because I'd seen in the Bible that I have whatever I say in faith, some days I would say out loud 20 times, "By His stripes, I was healed!"

In the midst of believing for my healing, the bank called. They had loaned me almost $2 million to build our new ministry center. Having heard about my heart attack, they were demanding immediate repayment on the balance of their loan. Even though we had repaid two-thirds of the loan in only five years, they were afraid of losing their money. When I told my banker that God had healed me, he just stared at me for a long time. Finally, he told me if I could get an insurance company to insure me for a million dollars, he would extend the loan five more years.

The insurance company required me to take a stress test and a CAT scan before they would insure me. When the results came back the doctors were so confused, they insisted I take another one. The second time the results came back the same. The doctors said to me, "We don't understand it. There is absolutely nothing wrong with your heart. You must have been misdiagnosed." All I can say is, God gave me a brand new heart!

Many times since then, I've been tempted to fear when I felt symptoms in my body. But I've learned to enter the rest of God by faith and proclaim Psalm 91 over my life: "With long life and many blessings God will show me His salvation!"

If you need healing today, I want you to know we serve a God who still performs miracles. He is able to do for you what even the best doctors can't. Nothing is impossible for Him, if you'll only believe His Word. So open your Bible and start building your faith. Read and meditate on as many of the healing promises in the Word of God as you can. Hide those scriptures in your heart and confess them over your body.

When you take your situation to the Lord in prayer, believe when you pray that by the stripes Jesus bore, you were healed. Forgive anyone who has wronged you as Jesus instructed. Then receive your healing, knowing that according to your faith, it shall be done for you!

A NEW CALLING

After I received my miracle, my whole life changed again. In 1993, during a time of prayer and fasting, God called me to teach and preach His Word. He explained to me that because of the increased revelation I'd received, He was requiring more of me. Luke 12:48 confirms this: "For everyone to whom much is given, of him shall much be required...."

My new calling didn't come as a total surprise. I'd been moving that direction for a while. In the beginning of my ministry, all I understood was salvation, so that's what I'd shared at our concerts. But as I grew in the knowledge of the Lord, my sharing times became longer and deeper. The more of God's wisdom I received, the more I desired to teach it. The joy of seeing lives changed was and is magnificent! Although it was slow and subtle, at one point I realized I was getting more satisfaction from ministering the Word than from being a musician, the only dream I had ever known.

With a fresh mission in front of me, the Lord instructed me to pass along my former call to my son-in-law, Peter Furler. He had a band called the *Newsboys*. God told me I could pray for him and transfer to him the power of God that had been on my life for youth evangelism if he was willing to receive it. Well, I did, and he did, and the *Newsboys* became bold witnesses for Christ all over the world!

Today I live in Texas where I am learning more about how to live by faith and walk in love from my spiritual parents, Kenneth and Gloria Copeland. I attend Eagle Mountain International Church and my pastors are George and Terri Pearsons, Kenneth's son-in-law and daughter. Mylon Le Fevre Ministries is submitted to their spiritual covering. As a result, the Blessing of the Lord as promised in Deuteronomy 28 is a reality in my life. God has overtaken me with His goodness!

Please understand, I'm not blessed because I'm anybody special. God loves everyone the same. He is no respecter of persons. It's His will to fill everybody's life with His goodness. He wants us all to be extraordinarily blessed so that we can bless others. But, according to the Word, God isn't the One who determines how much blessing we receive—we are!

It's our choices that make the difference.

God said, "Today I have given you the choice between life and death, between blessings and curses...choose life, that you and your descendants might live!" (Deuteronomy 39:19 NLT). If you choose to trust and obey God, the windows of heaven will open over your life and the blessings of God will pour out upon you as you live for the Lord. On the other hand, if you choose to ignore God and His commandments, you open yourself up to the power of your enemy. Make no mistake about it, the devil is real and he wants nothing more than to destroy your life, as he almost destroyed mine!

To learn more about making right choices according to the Word and experience God's goodness in your life, please refer to my book, *How Blessed Do You Want to Be?*

GETTING BACK WHAT I LOST

When I moved to Texas, one of the greatest blessings that overtook me was my marriage to the love of my life, Christi. What a wonderful surprise that was!

I'd married before in my youth, when I was living the rock and roll lifestyle. With everything that was going on in my life back then, the marriage had been difficult. After I gave my life to Jesus in 1980, it had seemed for a while that things were getting better so I'd continued to believe God for many years that His love would reign in that relationship. But He never violates anyone's will. Ultimately, different choices were made and the marriage ended.

Although those were tumultuous years, in the midst of them God gave me my precious, wonderful daughter, Summer. She was 11 years old when I surrendered my life to Jesus, so she'd seen her daddy living in sin for years. But when I asked her to forgive me, she did. She has loved the Lord and endeavored to do His will since childhood. She is now in the ministry with her husband, Peter Furler, a mighty man of God. They are taking the Good News to this generation. I am so proud of them. They both have chosen life and their blessed lives and marriage are proof that we serve a good God!

My daughter, Summer, and her husband, Peter Furler

Despite a failed marriage, I knew that our God is a God of restoration. He's promised to give back to us the years that sin has stolen from us (Joel 2:25). He's given His Word that He will replenish what we lost during the time we wasted living in disobedience to Him. If you're still young that may not mean much to you. But if you have some miles on you like I do, this is great news: God is ready, willing, and able to renew our youth!

He's proven that to me in my marriage to Christi. She walked away from her successful career in interior design to answer the call of God with me. We married in 1998 and I can truly say that we've experienced holy matrimony. Thank God, I finally know what it means to have true love!

Christi and I have the power of agreement and we are seeing our prayers answered every day. God's promises haven't all come to pass exactly when or how we thought they would, but we know by faith they are all ours— whether we've seen them fulfilled yet or not.

With Kenneth & Gloria Copeland who officiated our ceremony and ordained Christi into full-time ministry on our wedding day!

Galatians 6:9 encourages us not to get weary in believing and doing the right thing, for the right reason, with the right attitude, because in "due season we shall reap" if we don't give up. So Christi and I just keep on keeping on with God!

Upper Right: *Ministering at a prison with Mike Barber Ministries*

Lower Left: *"When I was in prison you came and visited me."*

Lower Right: *At Texas Motor Speedway for a NASCAR chapel service*

We travel everywhere together sharing the good news of the gospel of Jesus Christ. In the last few years we've ministered to millions on TV and the Internet. We've taught in hundreds of churches, as well as sharing God's Word at NASCAR, NFL, and NBA chapel services. In addition to ministering throughout the United States, we've preached around the world in such countries as Russia, Australia, Canada, Israel, the Philippines, and Mexico.

As we live out our God-given dream, our desire is to evangelize the world, minister to the Church, and disciple Christians. We want to proclaim to every nation that the Word of God is true and He will perform it for whoever believes it!

HEROES OF FAITH

Upper Left: Pastor John Osteen of Lakewood Church; the first time I ever preached! **Upper Right:** With Rev. Kenneth and Oretha Hagin **Lower Left:** Ministering on TBN with Kenneth & Gloria Copeland **Lower Right:** Singing with Bill Gaither & my momma

Upper Left: *Ministering at our home church, EMIC*

Lower Left: *Madison Square Garden*

TELEVISED MINISTRY
TBN Network

Upper Right: *Christi ministering at our home church, EMIC*

Lower Right: *Daystar Network*

CHAPTER TEN

LIVING THE ABUNDANT LIFE

MORNING STAR

Lord, here I stand before you on my knees
So Jesus help me please
I want to be just like you
I will, I will cause it's your will
I can, I can do anything
Because of what you've done for me

So I'll praise you till the mountains reach the sky
Till the rivers all run dry
Because of what you've done for me
And I'll praise you with my lips and my guitar
Cause you are my morning star, oh Jesus

So now I bow before you in my heart
So Jesus make me smart
Enough to just be humble
I will, I will be holy too
And I can I can because of you
Because of what you've done for me

Lyrics by Mylon Le Fevre
Angel Band Music
Used by permission

Today is the first day of forever! So let me ask you, *How do you want your forever to be?*

God wants it to be wonderful. He desires, as Jesus said in The Lord's Prayer, for His will to be done in your life on earth as it is in heaven. Think of it: days of heaven on earth at your house! Wouldn't that be great? Of course it would; and God has made it possible because He is good and His mercy endures forever.

The whole purpose of this book is to encourage you to see what the Lord's mercy and goodness can do for you. That's why I've shared my testimony with you. It proves that God can take a life that's been wrecked by sin and totally transform it.

I'm a blessed man today because of the goodness of God. My wife and daughter really love and honor me. I'm surrounded with the most wonderful friends you can imagine. I've experienced the joy of leading hundreds of thousands of people into a loving relationship with the Son of God. I've been privileged to see with my own eyes, the supernatural power of God healing, restoring, and liberating hurt people. I can truthfully say, as I approach 70 years old, that all my dreams either already have or are coming true. I live in my dream home and drive my dream car. God has even given me my dream motorcycle. I can truly testify that the Lord has overtaken me with His blessings.

Why am I so blessed? Do I deserve it? Did I earn God's love, mercy, favor, and peace? No, that's impossible. Was it my hard work and self-discipline? No way. Was it just good luck? There's no such thing. Was it because I'm so highly intelligent? Everyone who really knows me would laugh at that idea!

Ministering in Jerusalem

The most intelligent thing I've ever done was to humble myself before God and receive His Son, Jesus, as my Lord and Master. After that, what I had to do was simple: Just treat God like He is God. Honor Him, trust Him, and believe Him. Read His Word and do what He says. Seek first His Kingdom and His righteousness (His right way of thinking, talking, acting, and reacting). Relate to Him as if He's more important than anything else on this planet, because He is. He created it and every good thing that ever happens in life comes from Him.

CHOOSE YOUR FUTURE

As I've already said, God has given us all the opportunity to choose our future. He has set before us life and death, the blessing and the curse (Deuteronomy 30:19). Because He's merciful and He's seen the bad choices we've made in the past, He's given us a hint about the choices we should make from here on out. He's said, "Now **choose life** that you and your descendants may live."

I made that choice when I gave my life to Jesus over 30 years ago, and I've continued to make it every day by endeavoring to live in obedience to God's Word. As a result, I've enjoyed God's favor, provision, and protection. I'm not saying I haven't made mistakes or been through fiery tests and trials. I've faced plenty of them. I created some messes in my life during the years I ignored God's Word that took years to fix. But, over time, God has delivered me out of them all!

My experience isn't unique, either. I have been around the world many times and I've seen that God is good to everyone who continues to trust Him through the tests of life. His blessings in the lives of all His people are exponential. That's why I can tell you with confidence, the longer you serve God, the more blessed you will be! As you read and think about His Word, your mind will be renewed with His wisdom. As you show Him the reverence and honor He deserves, He will bless you so you can bless others. As you bless others, He will be able to trust you with more...and more...and more.

It's a wonderful life and you can have it. Every day you get to choose!

WHAT WILL YOU SAY?

Maybe right now you're just getting started. Maybe you're in the same situation I was that night at the concert when I made Jesus my Lord, and you're just beginning to choose life. If so, here's something you need to know: Revelation 12:11 says that Satan is defeated by the blood of the Lamb and the word of our testimony. The Lamb of God is His Son, Jesus, and our testimony is telling others what He has done for us. So your life of victory depends on telling somebody what God has done, and is doing, for you!

I realize you may be facing great challenges in your life right now. You may be in a situation that looks hopeless. But I believe as you've read my life story, you've learned there is no such thing as a hopeless situation with God. You've seen how the Lord delivered me out of a horrible pit of fear, rage, depression, drugs, divorce, and poverty, and you know He will do the same for you.

Although hearing God's Word is what gives us faith, sometimes a testimony inspires us to put our faith into action. That's my prayer for this book. I pray it's inspired you to use your faith to believe God for your miracle breakthrough. And even though you may not be able to see that breakthrough yet with your physical eyes, you can testify about it. You can tell others what the Bible says about your life. You can declare, as Psalm 103 does:

> *Bless the LORD, O my soul; And all that is within me, bless His holy name! Bless the LORD, O my soul, And forget not all His benefits: Who forgives all your iniquities, Who heals all your diseases, Who redeems your life from destruction, Who crowns you with lovingkindness and tender mercies, Who satisfies your mouth with good things, So that your youth is renewed like the eagle's…*
>
> *He has not dealt with us according to our sins, Nor punished us according to our iniquities. For as the heavens are high above the earth, So great is His mercy toward those who fear Him; As far as the east is from the west, So far has He removed our transgressions from us. As a father pities his children, So the LORD pities those who fear Him. For He knows our frame; He remembers that we are dust. (verses 1-5, 10-14 NKJV)*

GOSPEL MUSIC ASSOCIATION
AND
GEORGIA MUSIC HALL OF FAME CEREMONIES

Above Left: The Newsboys *backed me on my songs* "Gospel Ship" *and* "Without Him"
Above Right: *With my wife, Christi, my daughter, Summer, and son-in-law, Peter Furler*

Opposite page:
Upper Left: *With my sweet momma who was also inducted into the GMA & Georgia Music Hall of Fame*
Upper Right: *With our anointed pastors, George and Terri Pearsons of Eagle Mountain Intl. Church*
Lower Left: *Being accompanied on the piano by my musical mentor, Allen Toussaint*
Lower Right: *Being inducted by my brother Meurice Le Fevre and Allen Toussaint*

That's one of my favorite passages in the Bible. It's a perfect description of what Jesus has done for everyone who will believe and receive it. I believe we should quote it often because testifying is one of the ways we defeat the enemy in our lives. We should even personalize it by saying things like, "I'm forgiven! I'm healed! My life is crowned with God's love! My youth is renewed like the eagles!" You might feel awkward making those statements at first, but remember this:

THE WAY YOU DESCRIBE YOUR LIFE TO OTHERS ALL DAY EVERY DAY IS YOUR **TEST**-IMONY.

So from now on, watch what you say about yourself to others. When your family, friends, or co-workers ask you how things are going, keep in mind that every time you answer, you are being tested. How you testify determines whether the enemy of lack, discouragement, sickness, or fear is being exalted or defeated in your life!

If you don't know who you are in Christ, all you can say is how you feel and what you think. So grab your Bible and find out who you are and what you believe. Discover all the good things God has given you. Then you can testify and live in victory!

GOD IS NOT THE THIEF

To get a handle on just how much you've received if you've given your life to Jesus, check out Ephesians 1:3. It says that in Him we've been "blessed with every spiritual blessing in heavenly places." That means every single blessing heaven enjoys today, we can have at our house! In heaven, there's no grumbling and complaining about politics or the economy. There's no fussing and fighting, or going to sleep crying. There's no competition, lying, or manipulation. There's no fear, depression, discouragement, jealousy, or strife. In heaven, there is just the pleasure of the presence and goodness of God; basking in the light of His glory!

Can we really enjoy such heavenly goodness while we're still living on earth?

Yes! Jesus came so that we could have abundant life not just in the sweet by and by, but in the sometimes harsh reality of the rugged here and now. He came so that we could live each day according to God's perfect plan which is to prosper us and give us a bright hope and a future (Jeremiah 19:11). Even though the world around us experiences turmoil and poverty, ups and downs, God's goodness toward us remains constant. He is the same yesterday, today, and forever, and His prosperous plan for our lives never changes.

That's something you must really believe if you're going to fully trust God. You must understand that He is good and everything He does is good. His goodness is the foundation for faith. If you think He sometimes does bad things to His children, you will never trust Him with your whole life. You might give Him your sins and the things you're ashamed of, but you'll never give Him your hopes and dreams, your relationships, and your money.

Sometimes I hear people say things like, "God took my momma" or "God gave me cancer to teach me something." But that's just not true! Nowhere in the Bible did Jesus (who is the exact image of the Father) give someone a horrible sickness or disease to teach them a lesson. On the contrary, He did just the opposite. As the Bible says in Acts 10:38, Jesus "went about doing GOOD, and HEALING ALL that were oppressed of the devil."

Sickness and disease aren't blessings from heaven; they're oppression from the devil! He's the one who's behind every horrible attack on your life and freedom. Jesus said it's the thief who comes "to steal, and to kill, and to destroy" (John 10:10). God isn't a thief! So, if there is something bad going on in your life, He isn't the source of it. Any destruction going on in your family, health, or finances, can be traced back to the devil who caused it either directly or indirectly through somebody's bad choices.

It's important to get this straight because God said if you resist the devil he will flee from you. You won't resist him if you think his attacks are coming from God. So let there be no more confusion on this life-changing truth: GOD IS GOOD! The devil is bad!

SEE GOD'S GOODNESS IN THE LAND OF THE LIVING

To tell the truth about it, our God is so good that even in the midst of trying circumstances, He turns things in our favor. He causes ALL things to work together for the good of those who love Him and are called according to His purposes (Romans 8:28). If we understand that, we can have the same kind of confidence King David had.

Page 104-*Riding on the high places with our friends!*

Page 105-*Enjoying God's creation on the mountaintop and in the sea*

When, in a tough situation, he responded by saying, "[What would have become of me] had I not BELIEVED (expected) THAT I WOULD SEE THE GOODNESS OF GOD *in the land of the living*!" (Psalm 27:13 AMP).

Notice, God wants to manifest His goodness *in the land of the living*. That means your life here on the earth. So please, take a moment right now to ask yourself: *What do I expect in my life, family, and health this year?* God wants you to expect His good things to happen in all those areas. That's why He said in His Word, "Beloved I wish above all things that you would prosper and be in health even as your soul prospers" (3 John 2).

God's will is for all of us, as His children, to prosper spirit, soul, body, and—yes—even financially! No matter how beaten up by sin we might have been in the past, He wants us to be blessed in every area of life. I know from experience how wonderful such whole-life blessing can be. My mind was so messed up from the drugs when I first received Jesus as my Lord and Savior in 1980, I couldn't even complete a sentence without spacing out and losing my concentration. But God's Word has renewed—and is still renewing—my mind. Now I teach in services every week quoting hundreds of scripture verses from memory.

My emotions were once a roller coaster but now my heart and mind are in perfect peace. I used to be driven to succeed at any cost but now I have learned to relax and be content. Today I rest in the perfect will of God as He overtakes me with His blessings! God has healed my physical body from all the years of abuse. He has given me double the honor where there was once shame. Now all I can say is "The Lord has done great things for me! I am filled with joy!" (Psalm 126:3).

By faith, you can say the same thing because God desires to manifest His goodness to you, too. Today, you can have:

Hope while surrounded with hopelessness.

Peace in the midst of chaos.

Joy in the midst of a depressed and discouraged world.

Financial increase and stability even in a bad economy.

Supernatural divine health, healing and wholeness.

Please know that you are not alone. While you were reading this book you were being prayed for. If we can serve you or be a blessing to you, you can contact us at www.mylon.org. It would be an honor for us to help you enjoy God's goodness in the land of the living!

If this book has helped you in any way, please consider passing it along to someone else you know who needs this information. The gospel is good news and it is free! So I encourage you to help somebody else and give it away.

JESUS IS LORD!

MYLON LE FEVRE MINISTRIES
P.O. BOX 822148
FT. WORTH, TX 76182
817-281-2700
www.mylon.org

CD TEACHING BY MYLON LE FEVRE

In these power-packed teachings you will learn:

True Love
Learning to Love Others the Way God Loves Us

- How walking in love opens the door to the blessed life
- You can live free of strife and contention with others
- Loving the way God loves keeps you in a place of protection, provision, peace and joy

How to Love the Rascals in Your Life
Walking in the Power of Love

- How to love those who are hard to love by faith
- Love can reign at your house
- You can have righteousness, peace and joy every day
- God wants you to be healthy, wealthy, and wise

How to Enjoy Being a Christian

- What stops God's Word from producing your blessings
- The fruit of the Spirit is the personality of Jesus
- Bearing this fruit is the key to answered prayer

Enjoying the Goodness of God in the Land of the Living

- God's plan is always to bless and prosper you
- God will fix whatever you give Him control of
- The Lord is your Shepherd (Supply), not the government or the economy

Your Breakthrough Is Right Under Your Nose

- How to release God's power
- Death and Life are in the power of the tongue
- How faith has to move your mouth before it will move your mountain

Freedom From Fear
How to dominate the spirit of fear

- Fear is a spirit, not an emotion
- You can live safely in God's secret place
- Jesus defeated Satan at Calvary
- Jesus offers you the keys to your safety

Holy Matrimony
by Mylon and Christi

"Whenever the word Holy is mentioned, God has to be involved. Holy matrimony can only be achieved when God's Word is the final word in your marriage. The Christ-like husband will be a blessed, loving, kind, wise, gentle, patient, peaceful, strong, and anointed man of God!"— **Mylon**

"My husband is my perfect gift chosen by God to help me to be like Jesus. God has anointed him to be the head of our home. Wives are instructed in the Word to honor their husbands with loving words and a gracious attitude. When we cheerfully receive God's instructions, He promises that we will receive from Him whatever we ask. Because God has proven His Word to Mylon and me, we have deep love in our marriage, peace in our home, and hilarious joy in our hearts!" —**Christi**

CD TEACHING BY CHRISTI LE FEVRE

In these anointed teachings you will learn:

Fed Up With Freaking Out

- Peace, What's the Big Deal?
- Is Perfect Peace Really Possible?
- The Power of Praise
- How to Get From Freakin' Out to Chillin' Out

Inside Information
How to Live the Good Life

- God wants you to enjoy the good life!
- You are anointed to overcome every challenge
- How to walk in supernatural knowledge and understanding

How to Be the Ultimate Woman
From God's Point of View

- You can have it all and still be a woman after God's own heart
- How to walk in the fullness of your calling
- How to receive everything God has purposed for your life

Don't Be a Sissy-Baby!
You are more than a conqueror

- Are women really the weaker sex?
- How to respond in faith when fear speaks
- God wants us to stay calm, cool, and collected
- How to finish our course with joy

MUSIC

Please note, music CD's have been digitally remastered. Not for collectors.

Bow Down

"I believe that the purpose of this worship CD is to open the door in the Spirit realm and usher you into His holy presence. As you bow your heart and mind and enter into His presence, you will find that in His presence there is fullness of joy!"

Mylon & Broken Heart
Greatest Hits

All the #1 hits from 1981-1988. Featuring: "Trains Up in the Sky," "Love God, Hate Sin," "Gospel Ship," "Morning Star," "Crack the Sky," "I Will Rejoice," and "The Warrior."

A Decade of Love

This is a collection of worshipful songs hand-picked by Mylon from his first 10 years of ministry with his band *Broken Heart*. Containing 15 songs gathered from six different projects, it contains more than history... it conveys Mylon's heart as an anointed worshipper.

Sheep in Wolves Clothing

This is Mylon's first #1 album. Musicians: Kerry Livgren from *Kansas;* Philip Bailey from *Earth, Wind & Fire;* Joe English from Paul McCartney and *Wings;* Rick Cua from the *Outlaws;* and Larry Norman. Songs include: "Trains Up in the Sky," "Gospel Ship," "The Warrior," and "Morning Star."

Social Media

Please connect with us at one or all of the following social media outlets:

www.facebook.com/MylonLeFevre   www.youtube.com/MylonLeFevreOfficial   vimeo.com/mylon

Today is the first day of forever...